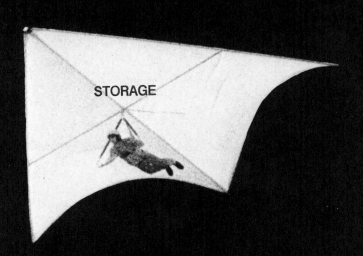

STORAGE

FLY

THE COMPLETE BOOK OF SKY SAILING

2 x 9/08 9/10

FLY

THE COMPLETE BOOK OF SKY SAILING

by Rick Carrier

McGraw-Hill Book Company
*New York   St. Louis   San Francisco
Düsseldorf   London   Mexico
Sydney   Toronto*

Other works by Rick Carrier
Books

DIVE: THE COMPLETE BOOK OF SKIN DIVING
ACTION CAMERA: SUPER EIGHT CASSETTE FILM MAKING
FOR THE BEGINNER
Feature Film
STRANGERS IN THE CITY

12345678RABP7987654

Library of Congress Cataloging in Publication Data

Carrier, Rick.
    Fly: the complete book of sky sailing.

    1. Gliding and soaring. I. Title. II. Title: Sky
sailing.
GV764.C37   797.5'5   74-4221
ISBN 0-07-010097-7

FLY: THE COMPLETE BOOK OF SKY
SAILING

To Francis M. and Gertrude Rogallo, the inventors of
the flexible wing glider, and all the pioneers of self-
powered flight.

My special thanks and gratitude to Fred Hills, Bob Mitchell, Marcy Katz, Steve Schreiber, Matthew Kardovich, Frank Matonti, and most especially to Kathy Matthews for her considerable editorial assistance.

For Lynn Ramsey, a most talented, remarkable woman.

Acknowledgments

I would like to express my extreme appreciation to the Chandelle™ Sky Sail Corporation for the help they extended to me in the preparation of this work and in teaching me to fly safely. To Don Stern, Jim Galbreath, Bill Sloatman, Don Beuch, Gordon Cummings, Keith Ealy and Colleen Charles, Mike Larson, Lee Sterrios, and all the other friends in Golden, Colorado, a grateful thank-you. I would also like to extend my hand to those of the United States Hang Gliding Association in California with special thanks to Bill Allen, Lloyd Lichter and the magazine *Ground Skimmer* for praiseworthy efforts in getting to the public safe and sound flying information. For the precision and clarity of his explanations of aerodynamic principles, I am most grateful to Richard ("Old Dog") Wolters, author of *The Art and Technique of Soaring.* To Pete Brock of Ultra Light, Kent Trimble of Manta, Gerry Ross of J. G. Aircraft, Donna Ross, editor of *Wings of Rogallo* newsletter, and Ed Vickery of *Sky Sports,* I extend a grateful thank you for helping me through difficult moments in understanding the depths of the technical side of sky sailing. To the flyers—Dave Kilbourne, Donnita Holland, Karen Rowley, Chris and Bob Wills, Kim Dawson, Mike Robertson, Tom Peghiny, and Dan Poynter, Bill Bennet, Taras Kiceniuk, Jr., Sam Alexander, Ed Butz, Captain Chuck Stall of Seagull, Mike Grey, Bob Balldeck, Al Waddell—I offer a humble thank you for inspiring me to reach for greater heights and insights into this dynamic sport, sky sailing. To those of you whom I have unintentionally missed in completing this manuscript, I offer my deepest gratitude and Godspeed.

Rick Carrier

Contents

To Rise into the Sky

FLY: It's a magical word. The thought of being able to lift from the earth and soar in the air has captured man's imagination since the beginnings of recorded history—and to what dramatic lengths we have gone to accomplish this adventure! We have flown to the moon and safely returned, and yet like some fundamental, unfulfilled desire, flying remains among the strongest of our recurring dreams.

Psychologists tell us that dreams of flying take many forms, from drifting over gently rolling countrysides to a highly accelerated fall into a frightening canyon. Whatever the dream, it often ends with a startled awakening that is not quickly forgotten.

One can entertain any number of explanations for the impact and frequency of dreams of flight. They range from the Freudian return to the floating fetal days inside the mother's womb to the subconscious desire to escape the pressing realities of daily existence. Dreams of flying are a common and regular phenomenon and occur with a haunting frequency that far surpasses other popular dreams such as floating beneath the sea or speeding across the face of the earth on high powered machines. It would seem that man's obsessive fascination with flight is as complex as it is instinctive.

When one thinks about the quantity and diversity of beings and objects to which man has given wings, a question invariably arises: Did any of these winged beings ever actually fly? And, if so, where, when and how? The famous legend of Icarus and Daedalus comes to mind. Daedalus, Icarus' father, fashioned a pair of wings out of feathers and wax, enabling both of them to fly off into the sky.

9

CARUS crashed to his death in the sea and Daedalus flew on to Sicily. So states the legend. It might be interesting to reexamine that story in the light of contemporary knowledge of powered and unpowered flight.

The adventure began in mythological times on the island of Crete in the Mediterranean Sea. Crete was ruled by a tyrant king named Minos and his wife Pasiphaë, a woman of great beauty and allure. Poseidon, the god of the sea, in a fit of outrage over one of her indiscreet amours, magically inseminated one of her ovaries with the semen of a bull. When the happy event arrived the newborn of the king and queen was blessed with the stout body of a boy and the head of a bull. He was called the Minotaur, and he grew up to be ferocious. Young human virgins were the mainstay of his diet.

In order to protect all the young virgins of Crete from extinction, clever King Minos procured these grisly meals from Athens in the form of a tribute.

King Minos was forced to imprison his unsightly son in a construction that was escape-proof, yet comfortable enough for the princely heir. To accomplish this difficult task, Minos made a contract with a brilliant architect and engineer from Athens named Daedalus, whose skill as a builder was facilitated by two of his inventions: the saw and the ax. So Daedalus and his teenage son Icarus went to Crete and successfully constructed for the king a fantastic prison. The labyrinth was a circular network of corridors, doors, ramps, stairs and dead ends that made escape impossible. The Minotaur was safely imprisoned, but after a time King Minos turned against Daedalus and placed both the inventor and his son in the labyrinth. Daedalus told his son, "Escape may be checked by water and land but the air and the sky are free." So he turned to his main talent: invention. He watched the hawks and gulls and marveled at their flying abilities and an idea was born: He'd escape from the labyrinth on wings.

Legend has led us to believe that Daedalus constructed his wings of wax and feathers, but that would hardly have been the solution for a brilliant engineer and architect. Let's speculate on a more realistic version of the legend. Daedalus knew bridge and truss design, stresses, load and shearing factors from his years of experience constructing stone and masonry temples. Being a practical man, he would have put hard engineering facts before dreams. To get off that island would require wings that would be capable of soaring with the ease of an eagle while carrying Daedalus' weight. The wings, or wing, must be light and strong; capable of being launched by one person; constructed from native materials; and they must work the first time out. A pretty big project to begin with, even for a genius like Daedalus.

The next step was the design. This required discovering the weights and measures of bird flight so he could transfer that information over to the wing he would build for himself. He captured one of the great soaring birds capable of cross-country flying, the vulture, and dissected it. He computed the wing area of the bird versus its weight and came up with the first fact. For every pound of weight you need, at the very least, 1 square foot of wing area. Being a masonry man and used to heavy loads, he probably doubled his findings when he got down to designing the wing, and came up with a real glider. If his weight was about 135 pounds he would have a wing overhead with about 270 square feet of surface. More than enough.

The wing would span at least 35 feet to incorporate the total square feet needed. His next step was to calculate the distance he needed to fly to reach the nearest land, Delos, 145 miles away.

By watching the griffon and the sea gull soar over the land and glide over the sea, Daedalus plotted their flight patterns and came up with his next bit of information. For cross-country flight the birds climb in successive warm air currents, or thermals, and glide to the next one, where the pattern is repeated. Flights by these birds of several hundred miles are not uncommon.

Daedalus, like any good engineer, probably built several models of his wing design to perfect its flying capabilities. Like any model builder, he no doubt used approximations of the final building materials—thus, wax and feathers instead of wood and fabric.

LABORING within the safety of the fearsome labyrinth, Daedalus swiftly moved ahead. Design after design was tested during the safe hours of darkness when all the island slept. Daedalus drew upon a storehouse of knowledge to incorporate all of the essential elements into a workable design. Finally he began to build a full-size wing. He utilized the Egyptian method of lamination to create the spars for the wings. For rigging lines he used carefully braided silk rope which had been strengthened by a coating of wax and pitch. By gluing thin slivers of tough olive wood together with marine bonding agents he created a skeleton that would eventually carry him back to safety.

An ordinary man, of course, would have been doomed to spend the rest of his life wandering the corridors and canyons of the labyrinth. Daedalus, however, had extensive knowledge of bridge, truss, and span design. He could cut the wood for the lamination process with his own brainchild, the saw. The wooden spars could be prestressed at the joints by being compressed between blocks of stone while the bonding agent dried. The bonding liquid could have been one of several agents available. Common varnish or shellac, composed of nothing more than dried lac bugs dissolved in alcohol, would have been a simple solution. Or Daedalus could have wrapped the laminate with thin linen threads and then coated the spar with a form of lacquer which the Persians, Romans, and Greeks used for their fancy boxes. The resulting spar would resemble the leaf spring found on trucks and automobiles today. The flexibility of the spar would allow the wing to breathe and flex under the heavy load factors that he would encounter on his aerial journey. To cover the wing he had available several materials, but the most likely candidate would be silk. Silk, which the Greeks called byssus, was light, strong and flexible. The final design no doubt resembled a cross between a simple mono-wing sky sail and the unfortunate vulture that Daedalus had dissected earlier. Things were beginning to look up. By placing man-made silk feathers on the wing tips, he found that the wing would maintain a steady course forward, the feathers acting as spoilers such as those found on a few of the contemporary sky sails.

Testing on the night breezes blowing in from the sea, Daedalus could begin working out the problem of the center of gravity. Considering the distance that he had to fly, it was obvious that he would need some sort of framework to hang on to. This cockpit would also have to be designed to hold his entire weight in a comfortable position. The idea of using wings attached to the flier's arms had long ago been discarded. Try to hold your arms out in front of you for twenty-five minutes without any weight attached and the absurdity of the winged-arm theory becomes apparent. In addition, during flight tests he would discover the need to shift his weight to change the direction of flight. This shifting would require some sort of simple swinging seat that could be hooked up to the wing and provide both flexibility and freedom.

A few final adjustments and Daedalus was ready to build a second wing for his son and teach him to fly. The difficulty of flying over the sea without thermals was solved by observing the wind currents of a raging storm, or mistral, that blew in from the deserts of the Sahara. Once he had learned the rudimentary steps of flying the wing, Daedalus must have reexamined the flight of birds, particularly the sea gull. During the storm he would have

he cliffs outside the labryinth were ideal testing locations for the wing designs. As the models spun into the sea or beach, the hermen probably hotly debated what they were and where they came from.

13

observed their style of takeoff in high winds. The gull simply spreads his wings and is forced aloft by the strength of the wind. Once airborne, the gull uses his natural flying ability to sweep, soar, and hover. All the time he is correcting and adjusting the angle of flight and changing the shape of his wing area by lengthening or shortening his wings at the point that would be our elbows. If the gull's wings were of a constant area and lacked the adjustability factor, the bird would not be able to navigate in heavy winds. He could soar and dive, but when hit with a strong gust he'd tumble through the sky like a piece of paper in a hurricane. Flight control was a real problem for Daedalus. He knew that to soar aloft and successfully escape the island he would face the same difficulties as the gulls. He reasoned as would a sailor out to sea in a storm: "Stay away from shore or the storm will blow you into the rocks." And so with Daedalus: "When flying in rough, windy weather stay as high as possible and don't fight the wind or you will crash into uncharted currents of air."

Icarus was waiting on the sidelines anxious for the initial flight. A typical adventurous youth, his concern was not for the mysteries of mechanics but for the glory of taking to the air. Daedalus continually postponed the escape, coaching and instructing Icarus in the fine points of flight. Icarus was restless and impatient. It was finally a natural catastrophe that forced the long-awaited launch.

Earthquakes are common to the areas surrounding the Mediterranean. One morning on the island of Crete, Daedalus and Icarus were awakened by a shower of rocks and rubble crashing down around them. The labyrinth was well constructed. While all the other buildings were tumbling down like so many block houses, it stood firm, and the Minotaur remained a prisoner. The wind accompanying the earthquake was fierce but steady. It was rushing across the island on heavy rain-filled clouds. Daedalus and Icarus rigged their wings, tightened the support lines, and out to the edge of the cliff they went. Daedalus' final instructions to Icarus were shouted into the wind: "Fly into the wind until you gain altitude. Forget about your direction and keep the nose into the wind. If you get your back to the wind before you gain altitude, you'll crash. Once you're flying high, head for the island of Delos. With this hard wind at our backs we'll make it for sure." Before Daedalus could finish, Icarus hooked up his harness and, ignoring any further words from Daedalus, put the nose of his wing into the wind and was immediately swept into the sky. Daedalus gasped as his son shot like an arrow into the clouds. With a wing span of 35 feet and a wind force of 30 or 40 miles per hour, Icarus must have reached nearly a 100 feet in just a few seconds.

And so the sky sail was a success. Daedalus followed his son into the clouds and, filled with elation, escaped the earth, the labyrinth, and the confines of mortal man. Icarus was to learn the hard way about the dangers of daredevil flying and the pitfalls of youthful impetuosity, but the glory of that brief, fantastic flight might well have been worth the cost of an earthbound future.

The speculation that Daedalus was the first inventor of the sky sail is, of course, fancy, but there is no doubt that the fascination with flight has been with man since the beginnings of time.

The history of the development of flight from the ancient myth of Icarus to the powerful jets of today is a tale of ingenuity, daring, and adventure.

Daedalus' flight, according to legend, reveals some interesting details. He flew from Crete to Delos in the Aegean Sea, a distance of approximately 145 air miles. Legend states that he recognized Delos from the air, but because his altitude must have been at least 10,000 feet, he was too high to land. The wind then took him on a westerly heading throughout the rest of the day and night. At dawn he landed in Sicily, approximately 640 air miles from Delos, which means that he traveled a total of about 785 miles. If he had remained airborne for twenty-one hours he would have averaged approximately 37 miles per hour. Contemporary sky sail flights have reached 10,000 feet and plans are now being made for flights of more than twenty-five hours duration.

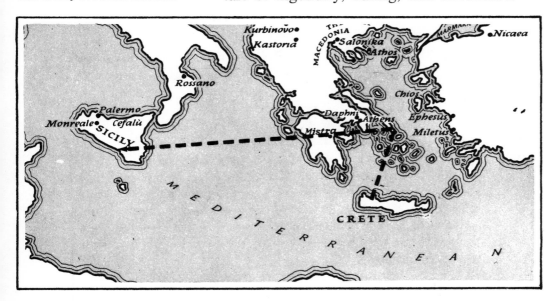

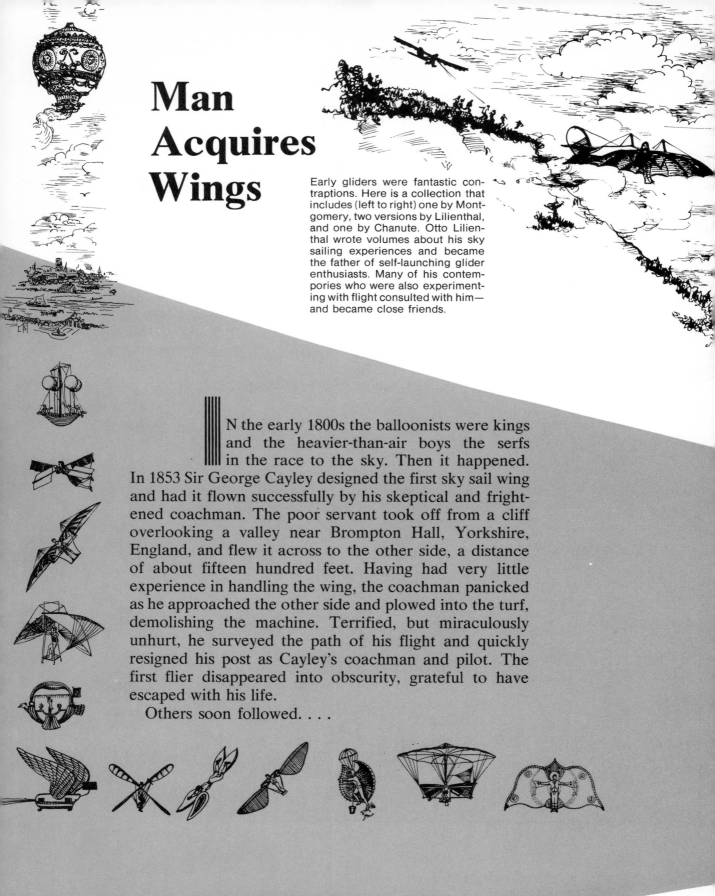

Man Acquires Wings

Early gliders were fantastic contraptions. Here is a collection that includes (left to right) one by Montgomery, two versions by Lilienthal, and one by Chanute. Otto Lilienthal wrote volumes about his sky sailing experiences and became the father of self-launching glider enthusiasts. Many of his contempories who were also experimenting with flight consulted with him—and became close friends.

IN the early 1800s the balloonists were kings and the heavier-than-air boys the serfs in the race to the sky. Then it happened. In 1853 Sir George Cayley designed the first sky sail wing and had it flown successfully by his skeptical and frightened coachman. The poor servant took off from a cliff overlooking a valley near Brompton Hall, Yorkshire, England, and flew it across to the other side, a distance of about fifteen hundred feet. Having had very little experience in handling the wing, the coachman panicked as he approached the other side and plowed into the turf, demolishing the machine. Terrified, but miraculously unhurt, he surveyed the path of his flight and quickly resigned his post as Cayley's coachman and pilot. The first flier disappeared into obscurity, grateful to have escaped with his life.

Others soon followed. . . .

THE heat of the 1800s brought the butterflies out of their cocoons. In a span of fifty years the dreamers were airborne. From Cayley's flight in 1853 to the Wrights' chilly December adventure in 1903 on Kill Devil Hills at Kitty Hawk, the wings of man tentatively unfolded, stretched, and finally achieved the heavens. The ghosts of all those who had failed helped support those fragile wood and fabric wings of the victors.

The men who achieved flight were a selfless lot. Nearly all of them died penniless. They applied for, and in many cases were granted, patents, but in the final analysis the early victors were eaten alive by the promoters and businessmen. Aviation became a carnival. Everyone tried to get into the act and the dreamers were left behind while technology took over center stage. Within the next sixty years, powered flight would take airmen to the moon. All but forgotten were the low and slow concepts of flight. Speed was macho. Speed was glory. Speed was everything.

Pioneers of Flight — Self Launch Gliders

1797	Garnerin Brothers	First successful parachute flight.
1853	Sir George Cayley	First aircraft glider launched.
1856	Le Bris	Developed lift function of wings, and flew one incorporating his design features.
1866	British Aeronautical Society founded	
1883	John J. Montgomery	First controlled flight in California.
1889	Otto Lilienthal	Made over 2000 flights in his glider monoplanes in Germany. Wrote extensively on flying.
1890	Clement Ader	Flew the "Ecole" in France.
1892	Louis Pierre Mouillard	Launched successfully in Egypt.
1893	Percy Pilcher	Flew at Cardoss, Scotland.
1895	Octave Chanute	Flew at Dune Park, Indiana. Made over 7000 flights.
(powered flight)		
1903	Wright Brothers	First powered flight at Kitty Hawk.

The Wright Brothers' Flyer I—the first powered heavier-than-air vehicle. It flew 120 feet in twelve seconds on its first powered flight at Kitty Hawk. Flyer I was powered by a four-cylinder engine and had an air frame made of wood and cotton.

The early glider enthusiasts counted on a lot of help from their friends. The group here is assisting a launch with elasticized (bungee) lines.

N the new age of speed not all the engineers and scientists were sucked into the gaping maws of the jet engine. A lonely few ignored the contrails in the sky and began thinking about quiet, gentle, unpowered soaring. There was little or no commercial value to their efforts, so they were left to spend their time unnoticed by all but a few enthusiasts. Small soaring clubs sprang up around the world and remained isolated and virtually anonymous. They whittled and polished their sailplanes to a fine degree of perfection. The planes were expensive to build and required crews and a towing vehicle to launch. But they set soaring records of hundreds of miles without the aid of engines. This new breed of birdman, the soaring pilot, turned to the works of the pioneers of the 1800s and began to study their observations and findings about gliding. This rediscovered wealth of information opened up a new avenue to sport flying. The engineers and technicians, after putting away their slide rules and calculus tables at the end of the day at the huge aircraft factories, went back to the shed or garage and began tinkering with wood and fabric. Soon new versions of the old designs appeared on the hills and beaches. Not many, but enough to begin to capture the imaginations of those who watched and marveled.

A recent photograph of Francis M. Rogallo. He and his wife invented the flexible wing.

One of the fascinated scientists was Francis M. Rogallo, an aeronautical research scientist employed by the Langley Research Center, a division of the National Advisory Committee for Aeronautics (soon to become NASA). Kite flying had been one of Rogallo's hobbies since childhood, and it was this hobby that inspired him to become an aeronautical engineer. When he applied his technical knowledge to his old hobby, he became dissatisfied with the kite designs of the past. He had other ideas. Rogallo was not a pilot but a thinker. Like da Vinci, he questioned the design of the conventional rigid wings on low speed aircraft. They were, in some cases, a hindrance. A rigid wing is impossible to dismantle. Moreover, they are subject to windstorm damage on the ground. In order to protect them one needs a large hangar for storage.

Rogallo drew diagram after diagram searching for a design for an aircraft wing that could be easily dismantled and stored in a bag. He wanted to combine the shape of the supersonic airplane with the collapsible canopy of the parachute. There were heady theoretical problems to overcome. The parachute had the fold-up qualities he was looking for, but its function was in opposition to the solution. The parachute was designed to cushion the inevitable fall of an object; it was not designed to glide or remain airborne for any great length of time.

Rogallo and his wife, Gertrude, began by making paper models and tossing them into the air like gliders. They attached threads to various locations on their models and twirled them about their living room. When one flew better than the others they made a larger version out of cloth and tested its flying qualities at their seashore summer cottage at Hampton Roads, Virginia. Back and forth they went between the two locations, testing model after model, adding new refinements and discarding the failures. They worked evenings and weekends and finally one of their experimental versions flew. They set about improving it. Weekends were no longer enough time. With a 36-inch fan Rogallo built a wind tunnel in their living room. They could now devote every free moment to refining that flying model. He drew plans for modifications and she cut the cloth and sewed the pieces together.

Francis M. Rogallo flies the original 1948 model of the flexible wing. From this flying model the first patents were granted.

In 1948 Mrs. Rogallo traced the latest drawing onto a left-over piece of a flowered chintz curtain. She cut it out and stitched it together. They then attached the necessary strings and raided their children's toy chest for a plastic astronaut. When the toy was tied to the strings on the model, Rogallo held the wing over his head and released his grip. It flew perfectly. And it flew consistently—in the wind tunnel, on the beach, in high and low winds. The Rogallos had invented a completely new aircraft design—the flexible wing. Many patents were filed. The

Model of the flexible wing with a curved and tapered inflated frame being tested in Langley wind tunnel.

Manned paraglider. This version of the Rogallo has been flown numerous times by several pilots. All flights succesful.

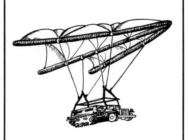

Tow gliders—military vehicles under tow suspended beneath a Rogallo wing.

Inflated frame paraglider—50-foot Rogallo carrying a weight of 3,000 lbs (Mercury capsule). Maneuvered by radio controls.

Photo reconnaissance drone. Photos of ground objects were taken with these radio controlled Marine Corps drones.

Fleep (flying jeep) test models have been flown for over twenty-five hours. The Ryan Aircraft Company is doing research on the design.

Thomas H Purcell, Jr., was among the first to fly a flex-wing airplane. Here he flies his flying boat design.

Emergency wings—a parachute substitute. An ejection seat with a jet engine attached enables the pilot to fly with a second set of wings.

first was granted in 1951, the second in 1956. A NASA report revealed: "The Rogallos have created a completely flexible lifting surface with a parachute-like tension structure in which the wing surface shape is maintained by the balance of forces between the air load on the surface and the tension in the suspension lines."

Rogallo tried to convince the aeronautical community that his flexible paraglider would be ideally suited as a reentry glider for NASA's space program. His words fell on deaf ears and little serious interest was shown. Then Russia launched Sputnik I and things began to happen. The Langley Committee on General Aerodynamics hurriedly requested Rogallo to move forward with his research and studies. From 1958 to 1972 NASA and their contractors and the Department of Defense spent over 100 million dollars on the application of the Rogallos' flexible wing invention. With the government spending a fortune on research and development, it wasn't long before news of the radically new wing concept leaked out. Versions of the Rogallos' flexible wing began to appear on the market place.

Air drop flexi-wing. A 4,000 sq ft wing carrying a loaded Gemini capsule weighing over 6,000 lbs. Radio guided to landing.

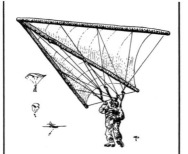

Precision paraglider being tested by the military. To be controlled by men and carried on the back like a parachute.

Paraglider to be lofted at an altitude of 700,000 feet by rocket to record micrometeoroid impacts on the sail.

Rocket booster recovery paraglider—radio controlled after separation from rocket package for safe earth return.

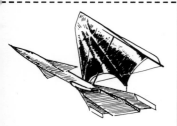

Flexi-wing applied to a multipassenger jet. If an accident occurs in flight, the Rogallo wing would deploy for a slow, safe landing.

Gliding parachute here being used for towing or drop-launching cargo. Precise landings are controlled by radio signals.

Rogallo wings on rocket. The wings are designed into the rocket assembly. The vanes on the top are for steering.

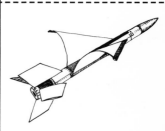

Foldable flexible wings. In descent the wings are unfolded for controlled glide to a chosen landing site.

The Sky Sail

To see a strange, delta-winged object soundlessly floating through the air with a person wiggling beneath it, as though held by the claws of a huge prehistoric bird, is an awesome sight indeed. Incredible as it may seem, it is an apparition that is occurring with increasing frequency throughout the country. On many occasions where this vision has appeared fluttering over a turnpike or expressway, motorists have jammed the roadways to get a better look. The spectators cluster around their parked cars and, shielding their eyes from the glaring sun, are oblivious to all entreaties from the police to move on. Finally, the fearless, smiling visitor from the sky marches up to the highway, his sail held high over his head, and breathlessly answers questions being hurled at him by the admiring spectators. The police mill about their patrol cars, shouting into crackling radios and scratching their heads, trying to figure out what law this birdman has broken. Happily, none.
So it has finally happened. . . . .

Man sailing aloft under his own power is no longer a dream.

Let's take a closer look at his wings. . . .

ONCE the flexible wing formula was released to the public by NASA the adventurers who wanted to fly quickly scaled down the government's findings to the smaller size that we see today. A new era of manned flight was born.

What did the blinking eyes and transistorized memory banks of the governments' computers discover that man up to this time had been unable to see? A remarkably simple diamond-shaped wing with twin conical sails that had the same flight characteristics regardless of its size and, when scaled down and mounted on a simple rigid frame, was inexpensive to make, completely portable by one person, and could be flown from any hill that had a gentle wind blowing up its slope.

When the early sky sailing innovators charged down a hill with their miniature versions of the Rogallo NASA wing held over their heads, they discovered that after only a few steps they were airborne. Not being experienced pilots, many of them simply held on and let the wing make its own flight path. In situations where they made a mistake and held the nose too high for too long the sail simply parachuted the pilot back to earth. They quickly began to discover the flight characteristics of the sail. It would level itself rather than stall out. It would fly straight forward rather than dip a wing and spiral down when caught in a cross wind. When the pilot shifted his weight, the sail would quickly respond by turning in the direction of the weight shift. These smaller sails had the same performance characteristics as the larger NASA Rogallo wings. In these early versions, the builders attached parallel bars to their sails. The pilots supported themselves by draping their arms over the bars. It wasn't until a year or two later that the triangular trapeze bar, which had been developed for water-ski-kite-fliers in Australia, replaced the bulky parallel bars and the swing seat emerged.

The success of these early crude sky sails stimulated a flurry of activity. The dreamers put their slide rules and pencils away and retired to the barn with their NASA statistics, their hacksaws, and drills. They emerged with bruised knuckles and a flying wing that would carry them

Vintage Rogallos—1971—fou of the original Rogallo fliers in the San Francisco bay area Left to right: Gerry Ross, Dav Kilbourne, Kent Shaw, and Donnita Holland line up to launch from Mission Hills. No tice the slack lower rigging ca bles and the absence of a king post on the top of the sails. De sign has come a long way since then.

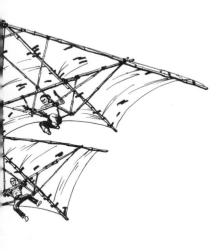

A sketch of Bob and Chris Wills low-and-slow flying their bamboo and plastic Rogallos. Notice the parallel bar controls and all that tape on the wings.

beyond their dreams; a flying wing that was to become the basic piece of equipment for the sport of hang gliding. Designers, engineers, and private companies began to file "improved" and "modified" versions of the Rogallo.

At the end of the sixties the Californians got hold of the Rogallo design, and it wasn't long until the surfers began to have some competition on the beaches. Bamboo and plastic versions of the Rogallo began to appear along the length of the California coastline. Their fliers had more guts than sense; their crafts seemed about as sturdy as toothpick constructions. But sandy beaches are forgiving crash sites, and the sport began to flourish. Each week brought more and more fliers to the launch sites. Torrey Pines, Redondo Beach, Playa del Ray became places to go to watch the crazy guys who jump off sand dunes holding huge kites over their heads.

The Rogallo sky sail was truly a self-soaring machine that was simple to construct and maintain. The wing was lightweight and had great strength combined with sensitive control. It flew very well.

25

SELF-LAUNCHING sky sails, ultra-lights, or hang gliders, as the new flying enthusiasts were calling them, are aircraft that fly without motors or any kind of external power other than nature's own forces—air and gravity—aided by the energy the pilot contributes on takeoff, in flight, and in landing. The goals the designers of these modified Rogallo flying machines set for themselves, and achieved, are remarkable indeed. They had mountains of research material on the flying techniques of powered flight to draw upon, but this vast store of information was useless for the pioneers of low and slow flying. They were forced to turn their backs on the commercial self-interest of contemporary powered flight and return to the basics of flying. They returned to the discoveries of those earlier adventurers in aviation—Lilienthal, Chanute, Montgomery, and the other pioneers of manned flight—whose basic preoccupation was the mastery of very low-speed aerodynamics and the fabrication techniques that were required for the design of ultra-light aircraft structures. The new hang glider pilot was also a pioneer. He had to re-discover for himself the basics of low and slow flying.

Donna and Gerry Ross fly tandem with their Rogallo over the water at Coyote Hills near San Francisco, California.

"NA-HE-LA-TA-TEH
(wind spirit)

Great Spirit, Grandfather, there is no other God but you,
maker of all things, hear me.
This day I come to ask permission from my winged brothers
of the air, that I too may fly as they do.
From my brother the Condor, teach me to soar as you do . . .
From my brother the Eagle, teach me to fly as high as you . . .
From my brother the Hawk, teach me to be alert and
quick as you are . . .
And from you, Spirit of the Winds, all I ask is
that you be kind to us.
To lift us into your arms and put us down gently,
for it is you that determines our day.
Mother Earth, just as the Wingeds of the Air your children,
land softly upon your face: I will try the same.
Great Spirit, Grandfather, watch over me and my brothers
as you watch over the Wingeds of the Air,
as we are about to join them in their domain.
With the soil from which all things are made of, and the wind
that will give us wings. I christen thee,
"Na-He-La Ta-Teh."
(Wind Spirit)

poem by
Crazy Bear Yaqui
1973 San Francisco
Wings of Rogallo Newsletter

The Rogallo Sky Sail

THE Rogallo wing is a feather plucked from the wings of Daedalus. Its design is deceptively simple, yet the flying ability of this delta sail is remarkable. Immediately upon launching a Rogallo wing, the air current passing across the gleaming nose plate picks up a track across the top and bottom of the loose fabric and quickly billows it out into a twin conical shape. This air current lifts the wing into the air. The Rogallo sail is half parachute and half glider. This dual personality makes it extremely stable at low flying speeds. At such low speeds, the wing has a tendency to resemble a leaf fluttering gently back to earth on a still autumn day. The soft landing is one of the main reasons this wing is the easiest craft to train and fly with. This facility of handling especially in landing maneuvers is why the Rogallo leads the field in quantity and quality of the sky sails being flown today.

28

I have seen a flier, on a still air day, come bombing in from a 1700-foot launch altitude with an air speed of 25 or 30 mph, and literally stop in the sky at 50 feet above ground. He can hang there motionless for what seems an eternity, pinned against the clouds like a huge Chinese dragonfly. The sail gently rocks back and forth in its straight path towards the ground until the flyer touches down at zero ground speed. His landing is so soft he never so much as raises a dust ball from the dry California desert floor. The pilots that perform this feat are not novices. They all have considerable experience with Rogallos. Yet it is hard to imagine the accuracy they display in their landings—particularly when you consider that the Rogallos depend entirely upon shifting of weight for speed and direction.

The Pilot

THE pilot trained to fly regular aircraft has little or no advantage over the novice in learning how to fly a Rogallo sky sail. Many people seem to think the sail is controlled by hanging onto the triangle-shaped trapezelike affair that extends below the sail. This is not the case. The flier is suspended from the gravitational center of the sail like a pendulum. He holds on to the control bar with a light touch if the sail has been properly trimmed, and tries to maintain this grip throughout his flight.

Sensitivity, not muscle power, is the key to being a successful sky sailor. Here is one of the youngest pilots, Hall Brock, age ten, flying a small version of one of his father's sky sails.

30

The Harness

Donna and Gerry Ross about to launch using their tandem-seat arrangement for flying.

The pilot is attached to the sail in one of three ways. The most popular is the swing seat held to the sail with a length of stout rope. The second, and considerably safer, choice is the seated harness. Finally, we have the prone harness. With this rig the flier is held in a horizontal position.

There is a lot of discussion among experienced fliers about which harness is the best, and the arguments will undoubtedly continue between prone and seated harness proponents without any resolution. The choice of what style of harness to use invariably becomes a personal selection. In the chapter on flying techniques, the harnesses and their various advantages are discussed at length. Without a harness it would be next to impossible to fly a Rogallo sail because only with a body attached to a wing can you provide weight shifting controls.

If you look closely at the illustrations on these pages you can see several methods of hooking up the harness to the sail. It is attached at the center of the sail and the pilot's weight, when in flight, is now completely transferred to this junction on the wing. This is one of the main reasons the Rogallo handles so well.

Now that the flier is hooked up to the sail, he is prepared to launch.

The prone harness

The simple swing seat

The seated harness

Control

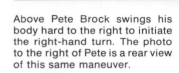

All the photographs here illustrate one of the four basic sky sail maneuvers, the right-hand turn as seen from different angles.

THE Rogallo sky sail has no movable controls, other than the flyer himself yet it can perform certain maneuvers such as landing with the an accuracy that approximates that of conventional gliders that do have movable controls, like the rigid wings (in this section) or the sleek sailplanes. The beautiful thing about the Rogallo delta wing sky sail —what separates it from all the other types of aircraft, which require a great deal of thinking and manual dexterity when flown—is that the Rogallos are flown and controlled by instinctive body motions alone.

Pilot weight shifting is the major controlling technique. A shift of his weight forward and back or side to side and the sail responds. Not quickly though. It takes a moment for the sail to react to the signal because of its slow flying speed.

Yet these four simple basic maneuvers, forward and back and side to side, when skillfully executed enable the pilot to fly his sail with virtual pinpoint accuracy. The experienced pilot can land on a dinner plate from a height of thousands of feet.

The opposite reaction is encountered on high-speed jets that only need relatively small control surfaces to make them dart around in the sky. With higher speeds, shorter reaction times are needed to change the flying direction of the aircraft.

Above Pete Brock swings his body hard to the right to initiate the right-hand turn. The photo to the right of Pete is a rear view of this same maneuver.

The sail to the right shows the right-hand turn as viewed from the bottom. To the far right, the sail high in the air is at the extreme limits of his right-hand turn and is rapidly losing altitude, while the other pilot makes his landing approach.

The pilot here has picked an ideal spot to ground skim—gentle slope, no trees or rocks. Note the sail plane dipping down into the valley in the background.

Performance

The Rogallo sky sail is a normally stable, powerless aircraft that flies at speeds of 18 to 25 mph to maintain its best cruising speed. At these speeds a Rogallo sky sail can remain airborne and soar from minutes to hours, depending on the flying wind conditions. It is similar to the flight of hawks or other heavy soaring birds. The sky sail has a still air rate of descent of 400 feet per minute. Flight characteristics of the sky sail are dependent on the weight of the flier in relation to the total wing area.

Taras Kiceniuk puts his Icarus V into a steep dive. Notice how he is positioned within the parallel bars of his craft.

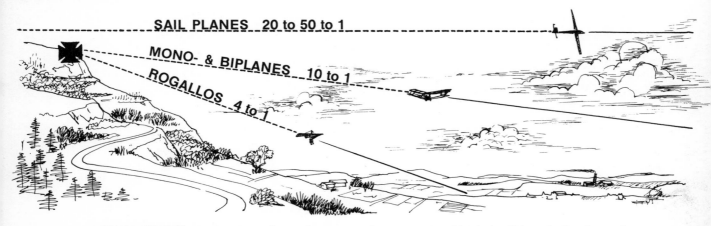

GLIDE ANGLES

SAIL PLANES 20 to 50 to 1

MONO- & BIPLANES 10 to 1

ROGALLOS 4 to 1

GLIDE ANGLES or ratios determine performance and are expressed by L/D, lift to drag ratio. Translated, it means the distance the glider will travel forward to the altitude it will lose in that forward flight. For example, for every four feet that the wing moves forward, it loses one foot of altitude.

Standard Rogallo

Modified Conical
note curved-wing edge

Styles

The Rogallo sky sail comes in four distinct styles—or configurations, as they are called in aviation terms. They are: the standard, the modified conical, the high aspect configuration, and the bastard (where the owners have made or added extreme modifications to the original design). Each of these four styles has distinct flying qualities. Not all of these qualities are necessarily safe or praiseworthy.

Bastard
note tail.

High Aspect
note angle of leading edge

Standard Rogallo Sky Sail

THE standard Rogallo is the work horse of sky sailing. It is stable and forgiving in most flying situations and is considered the safest of all the flying machines to learn on and to fly. Why is it the safest? Why is it the best of all the aircraft to learn with? These are questions that are most commonly asked.

The standard Rogallo sky sail is the safest and most popular sky sail because of its low flying speed and stability when flown in a variety of wind conditions. The Rogallo becomes stable and airworthy with a flying speed from 15 to 18 mph—the sum of your running speed plus wind velocity.

Pilots flying with these standard Rogallos have set quite a few records. They have flown above the 10,000-ft altitude level. They have remained airborne for over eight hours, been launched from mountains, cliffs, buildings, from balloons, from behind towing vehicles such as boats and cars and a variety of other launching techniques such as being shoved, or launch assisted by wing handlers. These extreme and sometimes outrageous flying feats do not represent the true picture of sky sailing. In most cases they give the public a false impression of the sport. Over 75% of the people who sky sail are ground-skimming flyers who never fly above 20 to 50 feet. Many of the above-mentioned launch procedures are extremely dangerous and should never be considered or attempted by any but the expert. The record flights only show the limits the Rogallos can reach when flown by expert pilots. The common use of the Rogallo wing is for flights that are launched from shallow slopes and last from three to thirty seconds and can be enjoyed in safety and comfort, with a minimum of risk to the pilot.

The joy of sky sailing is not measured by how high, how far, or how long one has flown but by the thrill and excitement received from the freedom and fun of each successful flight. Flying a sky sail is not restricted to the young and athletic. Accomplished pilot ages range from ten to sixty. Prior knowledge of aeronautics is unnecessary. Another aspect of the sport of sky sailing is that it can be enjoyed the year round. Some fliers say that flying in the winter, because of the density of the air, is better than in the summer. In addition, the atmospheric energy is free; the sky sail is a nonpollutant and requires no energy other than that which the pilot contributes, can be flown almost anywhere, and the basics of sky sailing can be acquired in a day and skilled flight in a few months. It is a relatively inexpensive sport. A professionally built sail costs about as much as an inexpensive motor cycle or a complete ski outfit. Prices range from about $250 to $700. Flying sites can usually be found locally. Any shallow hill with an elevation from 20 to 100 feet and a 7 to 10 mph consistent breeze blowing up its slope is suitable. It is a sport the entire family can enjoy.

One difference between the standard Rogallo and other sky sails is the angle at which the wings spread out from the nose of the craft. This apex angle ranges from 80° to 90°, which provides the best all-around flight stability for most flying conditions. This was one of the notable facts discovered by Dr. Rogallo. The other was the depth of the conical shape of the sail at the trailing edge when in flight. These are the two main differences that distinguish the standard Rogallo from all the others. The construction, materials for the air frame, the fabric and rigging cables are all virtually the same.

Standard Rogallo Sky Sail

In its construction, the standard has straight wing tubes and a cross bar. The keel tube is straight but has a slight upward bend at the tail only. This reflex adjusts the trim of the sail and gives it one of its stable flying qualities. Should this slight upward deflection be reversed, the sail would have a tendency to want to stay in a diving flight pattern regardless of how much compensation the pilot tried to exert against the flight of the sail. The adjustment of this upward deflection of the keel tube is discussed in the preflight section of this book.

All of the standard Rogallo sails available today from respectable manufacturers are basically the same. There are slight differences as shown in the two examples here.

The characteristics of the standard Rogallo sky sail can be summarized simply. It is light, compact, and has great strength; it is sensitive to control and easy for people of all age levels to fly; it is simple to carry either on one's shoulders or on top of a car; finally it is available in sizes to suit any pilot for nearly all flying conditions.

If a person wants to discover new outlets for his flying talents, he can join one of the many clubs that are springing up all over the country or subscribe to one of the excellent, informative publications that specialize in the sport. A comprehensive list of both can be found at the end of this book.

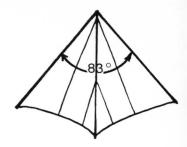

Of all the available sky sails, the Rogallo is by far the easiest to manage in all respects, and, accordingly, is the most popular. There are distinct differences among sky sail designs, and we will now explore them. The ones chosen in this section were selected from all of the various types available today because these aircraft best represent the uniquely different design features of each.

Data & drawings supplied by Chandelle Corporation, Denver, Colorado

SPECIFICATIONS

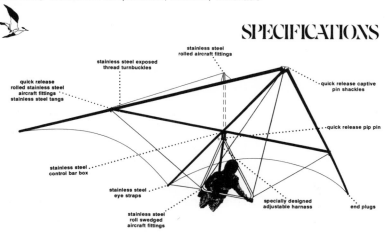

stainless steel rolled aircraft fittings
stainless steel exposed thread turnbuckles
quick release rolled stainless steel aircraft fittings stainless steel tangs
quick release captive pin shackles
quick release pip pin
stainless steel control bar box
stainless steel eye straps
specially designed adjustable harnass
end plugs
stainless steel roll swedged aircraft fittings

CHANDELLE SKY SAIL SPECIFICATION CHART

	LENGTH	HEIGHT	WEIGHT	WING SPAN	SAIL AREA	RECOMMENDED WEIGHT OF FLYER*
MODEL A	15 ft.	8 ft. 9 in.	31 lbs.	19.4 ft.	154 sq. ft.	85-105 lbs.
MODEL B	16 ft.	8 ft. 9 in.	32 lbs.	20.5 ft.	172 sq. ft.	106-125 lbs.
MODEL C	17 ft.	8 ft. 9 in.	33 lbs.	21.6 ft.	198 sq. ft.	126-150 lbs.
MODEL D	18 ft.	8 ft. 9 in.	34 lbs.	22.7 ft.	224 sq. ft.	151-190 lbs.
MODEL E	20 ft.	8 ft. 9 in.	36 lbs.	24.9 ft.	276 sq. ft.	191-230 lbs.

*The flyer weights are recommended for use at altitudes 6,000 ft. or above. Sail size will vary at lower altitudes and with a flyer's physical characteristics.

**The glide ratio for all Chandelle sails is about 4:1.

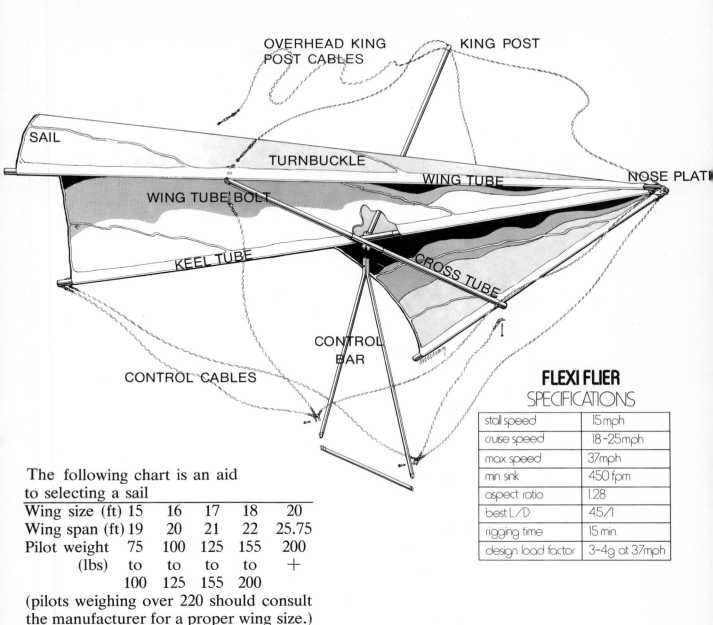

OVERHEAD KING
POST CABLES

KING POST

SAIL

TURNBUCKLE

WING TUBE

NOSE PLATE

WING TUBE BOLT

KEEL TUBE

CROSS TUBE

CONTROL
BAR

CONTROL CABLES

FLEXI FLIER
SPECIFICATIONS

stall speed	15 mph
cruise speed	18-25 mph
max. speed	37 mph
min. sink	450 fpm
aspect ratio	1.28
best L/D	4.5/1
rigging time	15 min.
design load factor	3-4g at 37 mph

The following chart is an aid
to selecting a sail

Wing size (ft)	15	16	17	18	20
Wing span (ft)	19	20	21	22	25.75
Pilot weight	75	100	125	155	200
(lbs)	to	to	to	to	+
	100	125	155	200	

(pilots weighing over 220 should consult
the manufacturer for a proper wing size.)

The sizes of sky sails are usually referred to by the length of the keel tube. In order to maintain
a safe margin of controlability while achieving maximum performance, the above pilot-weight
and keel-length should be consulted in selecting a sky sail.

Data supplied by Eipper-Formance Inc., Carson, California

Standard Rogallo

WING FABRIC. . . . Dacron is the fabric used on practically all the sky sails manufactured today. Other fabrics can be used, but only at the manufacturer's specifications. Under no circumstances should ordinary plastic or other materials be used to make or repair a sky sail wing. Safety is more important than convenience or cost.

PERFORMANCE. . . . 12 to 45 mph. Best cruising speed is 15 to 16 mph and will stall at about 9 mph. Takeoff speed 15 mph.

ASSEMBLY AND TAKE DOWN TIME . . . . 10 to 15 minutes.

AVAILABILITY See index under Manufacturers.

WEIGHT . . . . . . 35 to 40 lbs. The Rogallo sky sail comes in several sizes to compensate for the weight of each individual flier.

GLIDE RATIO . . . 4 to 1
The term 4 to 1 means the glider will fly 4 feet forward for every foot it sinks or descends.

CONSTRUCTION . . . Aircraft quality aluminum tubing and rigging cables (nico press or ball-swaged fittings tested to 1000 lbs break stress). All fittings are of the highest quality aircraft manufacture. There are no standard hardware store fittings used as original or replacement equipment or parts.

The Modified Conical Sky Sail

The term modified conical refers to the leading edges of the wing tubes. The wing tubes on these sails have a curve built into them by the manufacturer under exacting specifications. This curve affects the flying qualities of the sail, increases their glide angle slightly, and lowers their stalling speed. However (and this is debated heavily by the manufacturers) they seem to be more difficult to handle. It is advisable to learn to fly on a standard Rogallo.

The High Aspect Sky Sail

The high aspect sails differ from the standard Rogallo because of the increased angle of the wing tubes to the nose plate and the length of the keel tube. These angles on the high aspect sails range from 90° to over 100°. As the wing tube angle increases, the stability and flying characteristics are also drastically altered from that of the standard sail. Because the wing is now wider it is more difficult to handle in most maneuvers and demands more skill on the part of the pilot.

The Bastard Sky Sail

The bastard sails are basic Rogallo sails that their owners have drastically modified to include airframe changes, additional flaps, spoilers, flags, and questionable rudders. Their flying qualities are so peculiar that they should only be flown by their owners.

NOTE: To increase the wing's stability the designers of the bastard and the high aspect often add spoilers. These attachments are placed on the leading edge of the wing to concentrate the flow of air over the wing in order to prevent stalls when making turns. Once again, the reason that the designers changed the basic Rogallo design is to increase the glide angle. Increasing the glide angle enables the pilot to gain more forward distance for every foot of altitude lost. The high aspect and the bastard sails are not for students and should only be flown by expert, experienced pilots.

"I put my feet up in front of me on the front spar to reduce drag—when the seat is adjusted comfortably it is like sitting on a park bench for 48 minutes . . . ."

"As is mandatory for low-altitude ridge soaring (for safety reasons), I very carefully made all my turns *into* the wind, *away* from the ridge, sort of long figure 8's. After about thirty minutes I did get rather cold even with my windbreaker, mostly because wind was blowing back up my pant legs. I was able to remedy this by tucking my pants into my socks while in flight."

—Taras Kiceniuk

Note: Taras is a licensed glider pilot flying a FAA licensed glider.

The Rigid Wing Sky Sails

THE Rogallo delta wing glider does not have a monopoly on the sport of sky sailing, although it is responsible for the surging interest in flying. There is another breed of glider that has been swept along with the current enthusiasm, more complicated and in most cases more difficult to fly. The rigid wing mono- and biplanes are carving a niche in the new sport of sailing. Their outward appearance resembles World War I-vintage aircraft, but there the similarity stops.

The outward appearance of the rigid wings would lead one to think they fly in a different manner from the Rogallo design. In fact, they are similar in many ways. They fly in much the same manner as the delta wings, by weight shifting plus the addition of rudders to assist the plane in its flight beyond the simple body shift.

But in the process the rigid-wing designers have sacrificed many characteristics that are basic in the Rogallo delta wing: size, weight, self-launch capabilities, ease of care and maintenance and simplicity of operation. It takes more than a few days' training to safely handle a mono- or a biplane.

The rigid wings shown here are the best of the breed, but the future will unquestionably see more and more of this type of sky sail winging through the sky. Once a pilot has mastered the Rogallo, the rigid wings are a natural step to take—not to give up Rogallo flying, but to have an entirely different experience with flying.

Icarus Flying Wings

Icarus II and V were both designed by Taras Kiceniuk, Jr., a young Californian who not only builds but pilots these remarkable flying-wing aircraft with astounding skill. The II and V are similar in many ways, even though the II is a biplane and the V is a monoplane. What makes them similar is the wing design. Both of them have sharply swept back wings that angle up and back from the center. The wings have a constant chord (the distance from the leading, or front, edge to the trailing, or rear, edge of the wing) and individually controlled wing tip drag rudders.

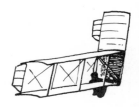

The function of these tip rudders is twofold. First, the rudders in their neutral position are slightly turned outward. This creates a slight amount of drag on the wing path which gives it more stability in its forward flight. Without them the ship would tend to yaw (see photo p. 64) back and forth, left and right, in normal flight, so they have been added to stop this action. Second, the rudders provide additional drag for banking and turning maneuvers. Each rudder is individually controlled from the pilot's position by twist grips or handles mounted on the parallel bars. The parallel bars surrounding the swing-seated pilot are not only a skeletal cockpit but also serve as controls for the plane. When he pushes forward, the nose goes up for climbing, down for a dive, left or right for turning.

Both planes are constructed of aircraft-quality aluminum tubing, with styrofoam and wood ribs that form the constant chord. Riveted aluminum plates secure all the parts together, which are then covered with dacron fabric that is heat shrunk and sprayed with several coats of aircraft dope to give it a final finish.

On the Icarus II aluminum tubing is used for the struts between the two wings, which are then braced with turnbuckle (adjustable) steel cables.

Control methods for these two ships are identical. Weight shifting adjusts the pitch. Since there are no ailerons, tip rudders help to control the sail when banking into turns.

It's interesting to observe the pilot's position while in flight. When airborne the flier simply lifts his feet up and hangs them over the parallel bars and relaxes until it's time to land. Not a very aesthetic posture, but nevertheless quite comfortable on long flights unless he happens to be flying low over trees or a cactus-riddled desert.

The landing speed of these rigid wings is about 16 mph, so putting one down can sometimes present a problem. (With the Rogallos a flier can touch down at zero ground speed.) A swift descent can present quite a hassle if the landing area is strewn with rocks, rusted barbed wire or other bone-racking hazards. I witnessed an exhibition at Sylmar, California that became a lesson for everyone.

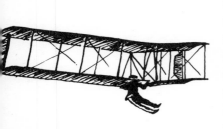

Here's what happened at the end of the flight. When the pilot came zipping in for his downwind landing, a kid on a bicycle was directly in his flight pattern, rubbernecking in the opposite direction while sucking away on a dripping popsicle. He was completely unaware of the onrushing wing bearing down on his head. The pilot's feet were dancing under the wing, trying to somehow get a slight push from the wind that would lift him over that kid, but to no avail. Perhaps it was premonition, the wind whistling in the wing's rigging or the frantic arm waving and shouts of the spectators that finally alarmed that kid. Whatever it was, he turned his head and looked over his

shoulder and saw what must have been a horrifying sight. The Icarus V was about to skewer him like a cocktail hors d'oeuvre. The pilot was unable to do anything but pray for the soul of that lad.

He held his legs as high as he could, knowing that he would clear the top of the boy's head by a few feet. If he felt he would bash into the boy, he could have pushed forward on the parallel bars and sailed up and over the obstacle and landed further on downrange. But he knew his ship and he knew he would miss, not by much, but enough to make a safe landing. The kid was unaware of what was going on in the mind of the pilot. His eyes bulged as the soggy popsicle plopped onto his stained T-shirt, and he hit the dirt in good marine tradition (no

SPECIFICATIONS

Icarus II—Flying Wing Biplane

Weight	55 lb.
Wingspan	30 ft with 200 sq ft of surface. Stressed for 3 Gs.
Pilot Weight . . .	210 lb estimated maximum.
Glide Ratio. . . .	8 to 10 to 1 depending pilot weight.
Construction . . .	Aluminum tubing covered with dacron and braced with $\frac{1}{16}''$ steel cables. Wood and styrofoam ribs. To build, about 200 man-hours.
Performance . . .	16 to 45 mph. Best cruising speed is 25 mph and will stall at about 16 mph. Takeoff speed 20 mph. Sink rate 1 meter or 3.37 feet per second.

46

doubt wetting his pants), just as the wind, buffeted by the Icarus, pushed the tall grasses surrounding the shivering prone boy into frantic twists as the glider slid close overhead. The pilot's legs dropped and, as his heels bit into the turf, windmilled frantically. About 50 feet down the runway the pilot got the wing stopped, and two spectators rushed out and helped him lug the Icarus off the landing target. I saw the kid with the bike out of the corner of my eye furiously pedaling off toward some secure place, no doubt where he could dry himself out.

There is something to learn from this near miss. Never allow anyone to stand in the landing pattern of any oncoming aircraft. It is a most dangerous place for both the spectator and the flyer.

Because sky sailing is a relatively new sport, fliers frequently attract a flock of curious spectators who may underestimate the dangers of standing in the landing zone of a sail. Whenever possible, it helps to have a friend at hand to clear the landing path.

...rus V—Flying Wing Monoplane

...ght . . . . 65 lb.

...gspan . . . . . 32 ft with a 5 ft chord, 160 sq ft of surface, stressed for 6 Gs.

...ot Weight . . . 210 lb estimated maximum.

...de Ratio . . . . 10 to 1 depending on pilot weight.

...struction . . . Aluminum tubing, 3/32″ steel cable braced and covered with fabric. It has a foam-sheet leading edge formed over aluminum ribs that create the 5 ft chord. About 200 hours to build.

...formance . . . 16 to 45 mph. Best cruising speed is 20 to 25 mph. Takeoff speed 16 mph. Sink rate 1 meter or 3.37 feet per second.

Quicksilver

Ultra Light Monoplane Sailplane

This versatile monoplane was designed by Bob Lovejoy of California. It has been well tested over many flights and a number of improvements have been incorporated into the final plane. Its construction is of aircraft aluminum tubing covered with a dacron skin. The flying qualities are similar to the Rogallo in that the control bar and weight shifts do most of the work. The high rudder at the rear of the craft has its control wires connected to the flier's swing seat and prevents the ship from yawing during turning maneuvers. Weighing in at 53 lb, quick assembly, fast take down, 8 to 1 glide ratio and one-man launch capabilities make this monoplane a good follow-up to the Rogallo wing. The Quicksilver is available in a kit form or ready made. It is perhaps the easiest of all the monoplanes to learn on. (See page 126 under Eipper Formance, Inc.)

The Quicksilver is a simple, light, monoplane design utilizing a ribbed wing of high efficiency. Good control and performance enable the advanced pilot to enjoy hours of gliding and soaring.

If the machine seems to stop in the air after a short climb, its stalling. Move legs forward to angle down and pick up speed. For full stall landings (which are not necessary), move the legs back just before touch down and the glider will flare up and stop its forward motion. To turn: swing weight in the direction desired.

On hard landings, the monoplanes can accidentally perform ground loops or half loops. Safety clothing is a must. Skids or wheels are there to help prevent these ground loops.

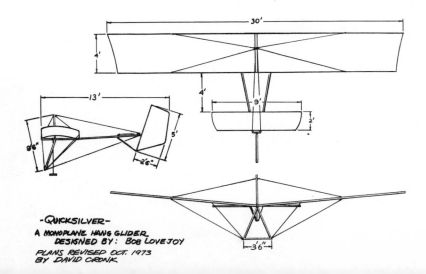

-QUICKSILVER-

A MONOPLANE HANG GLIDER
DESIGNED BY: BOB LOVEJOY
PLANS REVISED OCT. 1973
BY DAVID CRONK

QUICKSILVER B
SPECIFICATIONS

span	30 ft.
wing area	116 sq. ft.
aspect ratio	7.5
empty weight	56 lbs.
pilot weight	130–200 lbs.
des. load factor	3.5
stall speed	17 mph
cruise speed	22 mph
max. speed	32 mph
best L/D	7:1
min. sink	250 ft./min.
roll rate 45° to 45°	3.8 sec.
rigging time	15 min.

49

VJ 23 Swingwing Monoplane

VJ stands for the inventor-designer, Volmer Jensen.

The VJ 23 swingwing monoplane was designed by Californians Volmer Jensen and Irv Culver. It is perhaps the most sophisticated high-performance glider around. It is controlled by a "joy" stick (an aviation term left over from barnstorming pilots of the 20s and 30s) and a foot rudder bar that are conveniently located on the parallel bars suspended beneath the wing. The VJ 23 is licensed by the FAA and in order to fly one a pilot needs considerable flying experience. It has all the controls of a conventional glider. The elevator controls the pitch which makes you go up or down; it increases or decreases your speed. The ailerons control the roll putting the glider into a bank when turning. The rudder prevents the yaw during banking and makes the turn smooth and clean.

The wing of this glider is what sets it apart from all the others. Its great strength does away with the need for the external braces or support wires that are quite visible on the Icarus and Quicksilver models. The VJ 23 wing has a thin poplar plywood leading edge. Like the Icari gliders, the Swingwing can cut very tight circles without losing a lot of altitude. It has a glide ratio of 9 to 1 and can carry a pilot of up to 200 lb, although a lighter person is recommended.

The VJ 23 has an empty weight of 100 lb, making self-launching impossible. It is dismantled from the center of the wing and can be set up ready to fly in about a half an hour. The wheels are there to absorb some of the shock of hard landings and for tugging it back up a hill. It is 17 ft 5 in. long and has a 6 ft high rudder. This glider is not normally sold through retail outlets, but it can be built from plans with materials costing about $400. Kits and plans available from Volmer aircraft. (See page 126)

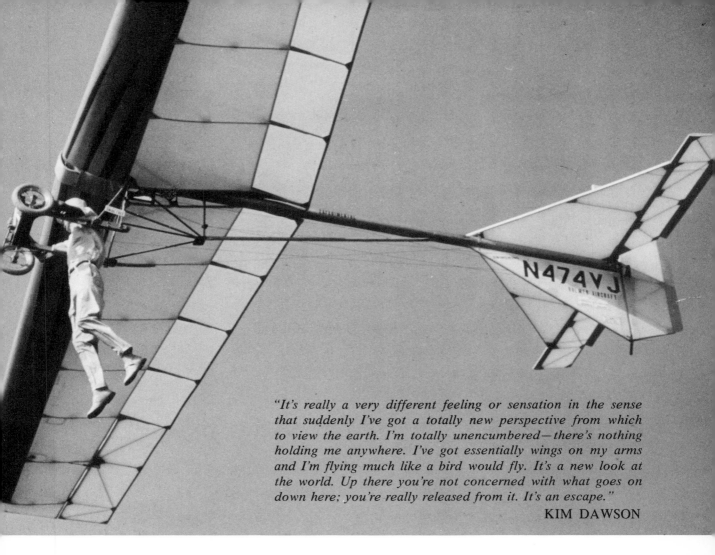

"It's really a very different feeling or sensation in the sense that suddenly I've got a totally new perspective from which to view the earth. I'm totally unencumbered—there's nothing holding me anywhere. I've got essentially wings on my arms and I'm flying much like a bird would fly. It's a new look at the world. Up there you're not concerned with what goes on down here; you're really released from it. It's an escape."

KIM DAWSON

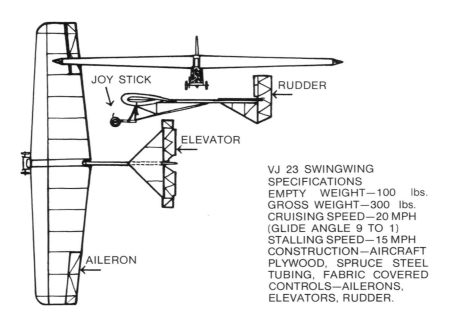

JOY STICK

RUDDER

ELEVATOR

AILERON

VJ 23 SWINGWING
SPECIFICATIONS
EMPTY WEIGHT—100 lbs.
GROSS WEIGHT—300 lbs.
CRUISING SPEED—20 MPH
(GLIDE ANGLE 9 TO 1)
STALLING SPEED—15 MPH
CONSTRUCTION—AIRCRAFT
PLYWOOD, SPRUCE STEEL
TUBING, FABRIC COVERED
CONTROLS—AILERONS,
ELEVATORS, RUDDER.

51

Roger Moore, the latest James Bond, receives instructions from one of the earliest pioneers of the sky sailing sport, Bill Bennett. The tow kite here is one specially built for towing by Delta Wing Kites.

Tow Sails

The tow kite is a speciality in that it is the only one in the family of sky sails that requires outside power to get off the ground. The required power is supplied in different ways. The most popular is towing the sail behind a speedboat or car. The need for this outside power adds an element of potential danger and thus the tow kite should be experimented with only under the guidance of carefully supervised, expert instruction. Otherwise, it can be downright deadly.

Delta-winged tow kites illustrated on these pages have an appearance similar to the Rogallos, but here the similarity ends. They are quite different. The design and strength considerations of a standard Rogallo are employed to accommodate the weight of the sail and the flyer during the gravitational stresses they encounter while in free flight or during hard landings. The tow sails and kites are beefed up in their engineering to handle

the additional strain applied to them by the towing vehicle. If a person were to hook up a self-launch, standard Rogallo to a tow line and start to pull it, the results would be disastrous. The sail would collapse into a twisted ball of wire, dacron and pretzelized aluminum tubing which would slam along with the pilot into the earth or sea at a velocity of about 35 to 40 miles per hour, the speed used to lift the tow kites into the air.

Mike Robertson of Ontario, Canada, snatches a swimmer in a display of skill that won him the tow sailing U.S. championship. Mike can't overemphasize the safety aspects of the sport to those who plan to fly the tow sails.

"Be forewarned that you should never hook up a tow cable to any kind of sky sail, unless that sail was specifically built for towing. Under no circumstances should a hang glider, especially a home-built model, be launched by a power tow. Nor do I recommend home building a delta wing (Rogallo) for towing, even for an able craftsman."

Mike Robertson
Former U.S. Champion
Tow Kite Flyer

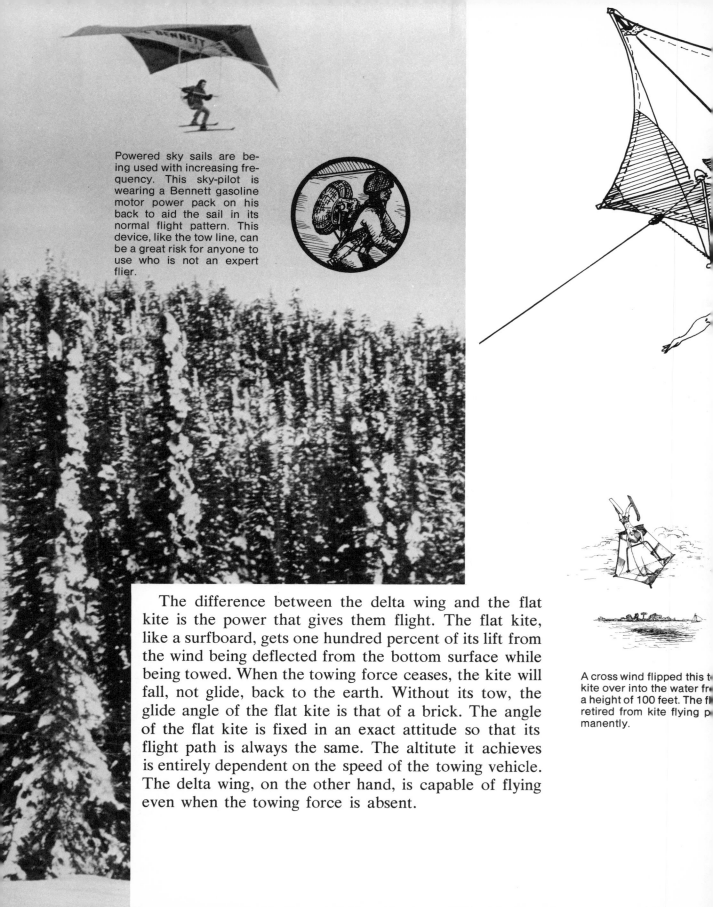

Powered sky sails are being used with increasing frequency. This sky-pilot is wearing a Bennett gasoline motor power pack on his back to aid the sail in its normal flight pattern. This device, like the tow line, can be a great risk for anyone to use who is not an expert flier.

A cross wind flipped this t‑ kite over into the water fr‑ a height of 100 feet. The f‑ retired from kite flying p‑ manently.

The difference between the delta wing and the flat kite is the power that gives them flight. The flat kite, like a surfboard, gets one hundred percent of its lift from the wind being deflected from the bottom surface while being towed. When the towing force ceases, the kite will fall, not glide, back to the earth. Without its tow, the glide angle of the flat kite is that of a brick. The angle of the flat kite is fixed in an exact attitude so that its flight path is always the same. The altitude it achieves is entirely dependent on the speed of the towing vehicle. The delta wing, on the other hand, is capable of flying even when the towing force is absent.

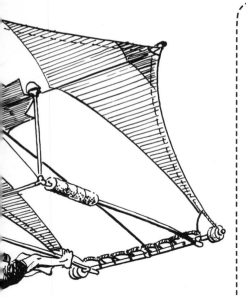

An Australian named Hargraves perfected the box kite for human flight. From there Bill Bennett brought the sport here, where it got extensive publicity in Florida. The sport of tow sailing is plagued with serious accidents and should only be tried by the expert.

Comparison of Tow Kites

	The Flat Kite	Delta Wing
Construction	Sail: polyurethane-coated nylon—slight stretch porous fabric Framework: aluminum tubing, steel cable support wires	Sail: dacron—non-stretch, non-porous Framework: aluminum tubing, steel cable suport wires
Pilot Control	Muscle power and body shifting	Body weight shifting only
Pilot Support	Webb harness attached to center of the trapeze bar (see illustration)	Swing seat attached to top of control bar triangle
Flyability	About 6 hours training required	4 to 6 hours training
Dimensions	From 8 by 10 to 13 by 15 feet	Sail area in sq ft to body weight only; a larger size requires elaborate safety precautions
Tow Line Attachment	Attached to a 4-point bridle of kite	Fastened to a quick release on an A-frame on the control bar
Tow Line Length and Tension	100–120 ft ⅜-inch braid 200–300 lbs pull	100–120 ft ⅜th inch braid Approximately 50 lbs in level flight
Air Speed Needed for Lift off	Approximately 35 mph	Approximately 25–30 mph
Attack Angle	45–50°	30° (can vary with each pilot)
Altitude	Limited by the speed of the boat and the length of tow line	As high as the flier can take it
Safety	Fly only after professional instruction; not for "self learning; can be dangerous if flown high.	Professional instruction a must
Build-It-Yourself	With detailed plans can be safely and easily built; will proably cost more than a factory built model.	Should not be attempted under any circumstances; there are no tolerances for error with the delta wing design

SOURCE: MIKE ROBERTSON

Here is Mike Robertson making a landing approach quite near the land—a most dangerous landing zone for any but the expert.

The Pilot

There are probably as many reasons to try hang gliding as there are fliers. Whatever your reasons, you should go through a basic preflight training procedure to give yourself a clear idea of the safest methods of flying before your first launch. Only a fool would fly a sail off a hill without knowledge of what it's all about. Good judgment in aviation is essential: it's what makes the pilot competent and the sport safe.

Your First Sky Sail

The student pilot should consider several factors when purchasing his first sky sail. These include safe, reliable construction, a standard design, light weight, and modest cost. If the student is to assemble the sail himself, he must consider how difficult the assembly will be, and the space and tools required for assembly. Most fliers recommend that the student learn on the standard Rogallo sky sail and avoid the rigid wing gliders and the high performance sky sails. The high performance glider looks good but is so difficult for the inexperienced flier to master that he will frequently become discouraged and give up on flying altogether. The wisest decision is to begin on the standard Rogallo and later move up to the more complicated sails.

Training Outline

The following outline covers the levels of training the student pilot should master in the given sequence:

"A" Level: Ground Preparation
   Theory of flight
   Setting up the sail
   Preflight check
      Sail fabric maintenance
      Protective clothing
   Ground Handling Part 1 (no running)
      Take down and neat wrap up of sail
      Transporting of sail
   Ground Handling Part 2 (running with the sail)
      Flare
      Left and right turns

"B" Level I: First Flight
   Introduction to the harness
   Review of ground handling runs
   Basic rules of flight
   Launch
   Landing

"B" Level II: Advancing up the Hill
   Introduction to Wind
   To the new pilot

"B" Level III: Advanced Maneuvers
   Launch
   Glide
   Turns
   Dive
   Specialized landings

"C" Level: High Altitude Flying
   Pilot judgment

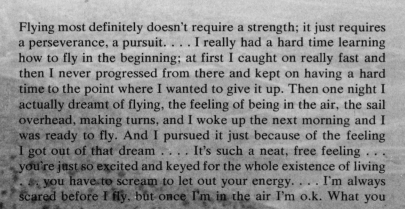

WHAT are the factors that keep a sky sail aloft? A hang glider flies because a combination of plastic fabric and aluminum tubing has been put together in a fashion that seems to defy one of nature's strongest forces, gravity.

"Theory of Flight," for the purposes of this book, really only refers to theory—or abstract principles—to the extent that an explanation of these principles will help the flier in actual practice. We are only concerned with principles insofar as they serve the flier's practical needs. Observation and experience will, finally, be the best teachers, but there are certain principles that you should familiarize yourself with before you take out your first sail.

The most important fact for a pilot to understand in

Flying most definitely doesn't require a strength; it just requires a perseverance, a pursuit. . . . I really had a hard time learning how to fly in the beginning; at first I caught on really fast and then I never progressed from there and kept on having a hard time to the point where I wanted to give it up. Then one night I actually dreamt of flying, the feeling of being in the air, the sail overhead, making turns, and I woke up the next morning and I was ready to fly. And I pursued it just because of the feeling I got out of that dream . . . . It's such a neat, free feeling . . . you're just so excited and keyed for the whole existence of living . . . you have to scream to let out your energy. . . . I'm always scared before I fly, but once I'm in the air I'm o.k. What you

# of Flight

order to handle his sail while in flight is the angle of attack. It is the basis for level flight as well as climbing and gliding, banking and turning, and, finally, stalling. Very briefly, angle of attack is the angle at which the wing meets the air. In order to understand the application of the idea of angle of attack and how and why it changes in real flight, we must first understand the forces at work.

In simplest terms, the sky sail holds itself up by pushing the air down. This is accomplished by the correct combination of a variety of forces, especially weight, lift, and drag. Weight is the downward pull of gravity that is converted into thrust or forward motion through the inclination of the flight path of the glider.

Lift is a quality of the wing's design that enables it to remain airborne. A sky sail sitting at the top of a hill is

have to do is look straight out—not at the ground—and that gets you over your fear of heights. It doesn't look high when you look way out to the horizon; you don't even think how high up you are. That's what you feel when you're sky sailing. Until you get good, then you look down and around. It becomes natural . . . . It's a rush to your whole body. When I landed after my first flight off Green Mountain, I was screaming so loud. I had no control over my body—not from fear but from sheer excitement. They heard me clear from the top of the mountain. . . . It's that sensation that keeps you flying.

Karen Rowley
Denver, Colorado ·1973

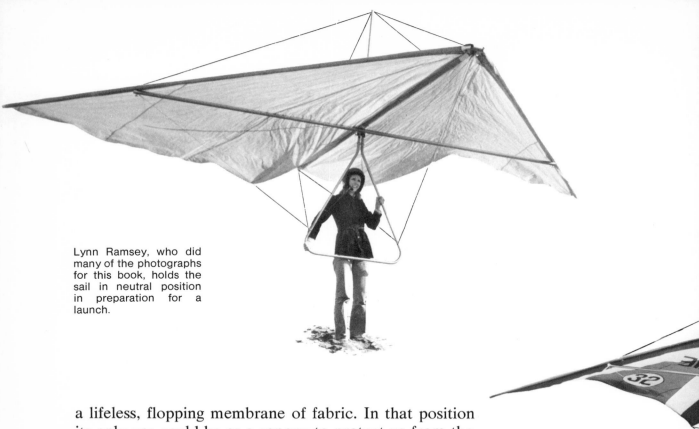

Lynn Ramsey, who did many of the photographs for this book, holds the sail in neutral position in preparation for a launch.

Bob Wills executes a perfect take-off and launch.

a lifeless, flopping membrane of fabric. In that position its only use could be as a canopy to protect us from the sun or rain. But pick it up, nose it into the wind, and start running with it, and it comes to life. When the fabric pops up and forms its twin conical shape, it becomes an efficient airfoil. As the air is forced over the nose plate it is split into two parts. One part is forced under the sail and the other up over the top. The air merges again after it reaches the trailing edge of the wing.

It's what happens in between that counts. The part that had to go over the top is forced to make a longer trip than its counterpart on the bottom. This means that the upper gust of air had to run like hell while the lower one simply trotted. Physicists call this race Bernoulli's principle or law; it states that the pressure of a gas or liquid decreases at the point where the speed increases. So the air above the sail exerts less pressure than the air below. The bottom air initiates a shoving contest with the top air, with the wing in between. Of course the slow-moving, heavier air beneath wins, and the sail is pushed up into the sky. This same principle is at work in the wing design of the rigid wing planes.

60

Drag—As the sky sail moves through the air it has forces trying to slow it down. It is important to reduce these forces whenever possible. The most obvious force is the turbulence of the air itself as the mass of sail, wires, and exposed pilot pushes through it. The design of the air frame and its appendages, such as the dangling pilot, can be changed, and changing these factors obviously affects the drag they impose on the flight. The configuration of the Rogallo sky sail is fixed, so the drag it creates is constant, but the pilot's body is another story. He contributes more than half the weight and a considerable portion of the drag on the ultralight sky sail. The drag that his body creates is changed mainly by means of the harness.

The other drag force, and the most important variable force from a practical standpoint, is the drag generated by the lift forces on the sail. This is the most important drag force because the pilot can vary it at will in flight by changing the angle of attack. Once again, the angle at which the wing meets the air is called the angle of attack. Theoretically, for every speed there is a corresponding angle that will produce just enough lift to hold the sail up at that speed.

Angle of attack is the angle at which the wing meets the air.

ANGLE OF ATTACK

Now that we understand some of the forces at work in flight, we can return to the angle of attack and discuss this most important concept more fully. The sky sail wing is basically an inclined plane. As the wing moves through the air at the normal cruising speed of 18 to 20 mph the nose of the sail is slightly elevated. The degree of this elevation is called the angle of attack. The wing generates lift, as mentioned, by exerting a downward force against the air it flies through. This downward force is counterbalanced by an upward force from the deflected air. This, once again, is lift. The lift will vary according to the angle of attack and the air speed.

Angle of attack can be easily observed on a sky sail because of its low flying speed. When the attack angle is high, the sail will slow down, the lift force will diminish, and the sail will begin to descend. At a certain high angle of attack, the sail will cease all forward motion and stall. When the angle of attack is lowered, the speed of the sail increases. The lift also increases because the air is being deflected downward with greater force.

It is vital that the student pilot become familiar with the feel of the sail at various angles of attack. The feel is different for each angle. At a high angle of attack the controls of the sail are weak because of the slow air speed and the lower air pressure on the bottom of the sail. At a low angle the control is stronger because of the higher speed. Experience will teach the student to judge the angle of attack by the feel of the control bar.

Zero angle of attack sail luffs
—no lift.

Medium high angle of attack is used for launching
slow speed—low lift.

Low angle of attack is used
when cruising
medium speed—medium lift.

LOW SPEED—High angle of attack.
Low lift. Air deflects off the bottom of the sail with little force.

HIGH SPEED—Low angle of attack.
High Lift. The air deflects off the bottom of the sail with the same force with which it first met the sail.

For every flying speed there is an angle of attack that will produce enough lift to keep the sail airborne.

ANGLE OF ATTACK CONTROL

As the pilot pushes out or pulls back on the control bar, he raises or lowers the nose of the sail. This movement adjusts the sail's angle of attack. With the nose held at a high angle of attack the sail will slow down and sink towards the earth. If the nose is raised into a high angle of attack when flying fast, the sail will climb. The sail then goes up or down not because of the angle of attack but because of a combination of air speed and angle of attack.

Neutral angle of attack is used
when diving.
High speed—high lift.

High angle of attack.
Sail stalls—no speed—no lift.

Negative angle of attack.
Reverse lift—sail is forced
down.

STALLS

Every sail has a speed below which it cannot be flown. When the sail drops below this speed, it stalls. The sail stalls because there is no air being deflected downward from the underneath surface of the sail. Drag increases, speed diminishes. The sail stalls. Lack of speed is the most common cause of a stall. When a pilot forces his sail into a severe angle of attack he stalls. When the wing meets the air at too great an angle of attack it tries to push the air down too sharply. The smooth air flow over the top of the sail breaks up into useless turbulence. The wing at this angle is unable to exert sufficient downward push to keep it airborne. In this condition the wing has enormous drag but little lift.

The triangular trapeze control bar determines the angle of attack of the sail. By pushing it out far enough a pilot can stall a sail at any speed. A sail stalls not only because the nose is too high but because of a severe angle of attack. In a steep turn the stalling speed will be much higher than in a level flight. The same is true during a sharp pull out from a dive. The sail will stall even at top speed if the nose is pushed up too quickly.

As the sail slows down in level flight, the pilot must increase his angle of attack to maintain enough lift to keep the sail in the air. As flying speed decreases to a certain point, even a very high angle of attack will not keep the wing up. Beyond this critical point the wing has stopped deflecting enough air down to sustain flight and

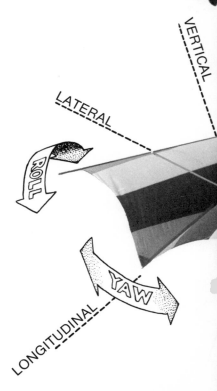

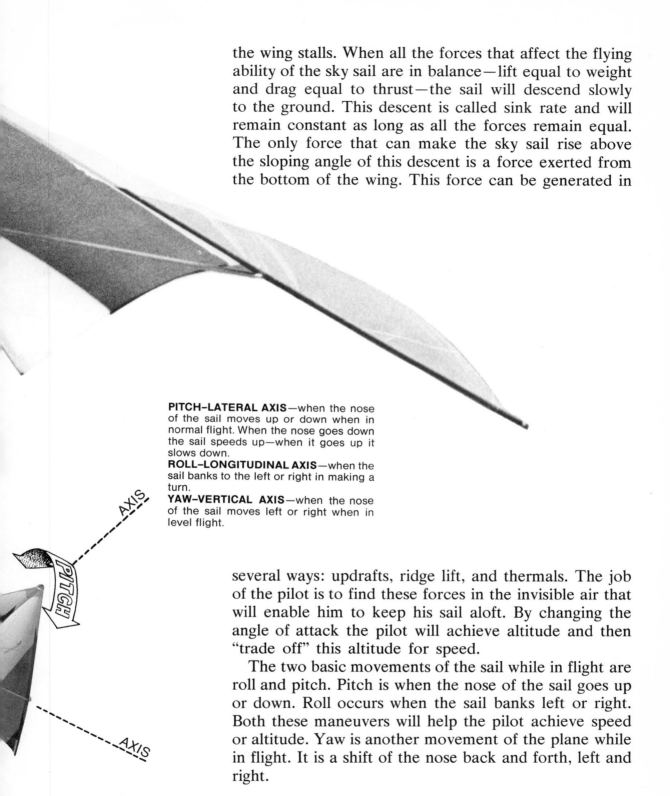

the wing stalls. When all the forces that affect the flying ability of the sky sail are in balance—lift equal to weight and drag equal to thrust—the sail will descend slowly to the ground. This descent is called sink rate and will remain constant as long as all the forces remain equal. The only force that can make the sky sail rise above the sloping angle of this descent is a force exerted from the bottom of the wing. This force can be generated in

PITCH–LATERAL AXIS—when the nose of the sail moves up or down when in normal flight. When the nose goes down the sail speeds up—when it goes up it slows down.
ROLL–LONGITUDINAL AXIS—when the sail banks to the left or right in making a turn.
YAW–VERTICAL AXIS—when the nose of the sail moves left or right when in level flight.

AXIS

PITCH

AXIS

AXIS

several ways: updrafts, ridge lift, and thermals. The job of the pilot is to find these forces in the invisible air that will enable him to keep his sail aloft. By changing the angle of attack the pilot will achieve altitude and then "trade off" this altitude for speed.

The two basic movements of the sail while in flight are roll and pitch. Pitch is when the nose of the sail goes up or down. Roll occurs when the sail banks left or right. Both these maneuvers will help the pilot achieve speed or altitude. Yaw is another movement of the plane while in flight. It is a shift of the nose back and forth, left and right.

Setting Up the Sky Sail

The sky sail is an aircraft. If it is built properly, it will safely support the flier for countless safe and successful flights. It requires very little maintenance if used properly. The pilot of a sky sail must nevertheless follow a set pattern of assembly and preflight check-out and a simple program of routine maintenance.

If there's a sky sail school near you, enroll in it. If there isn't—and that's the purpose of this book—order a sail from a reputable manufacturer (see manufacturers list, page 126) that conforms to your weight and physical requirements.

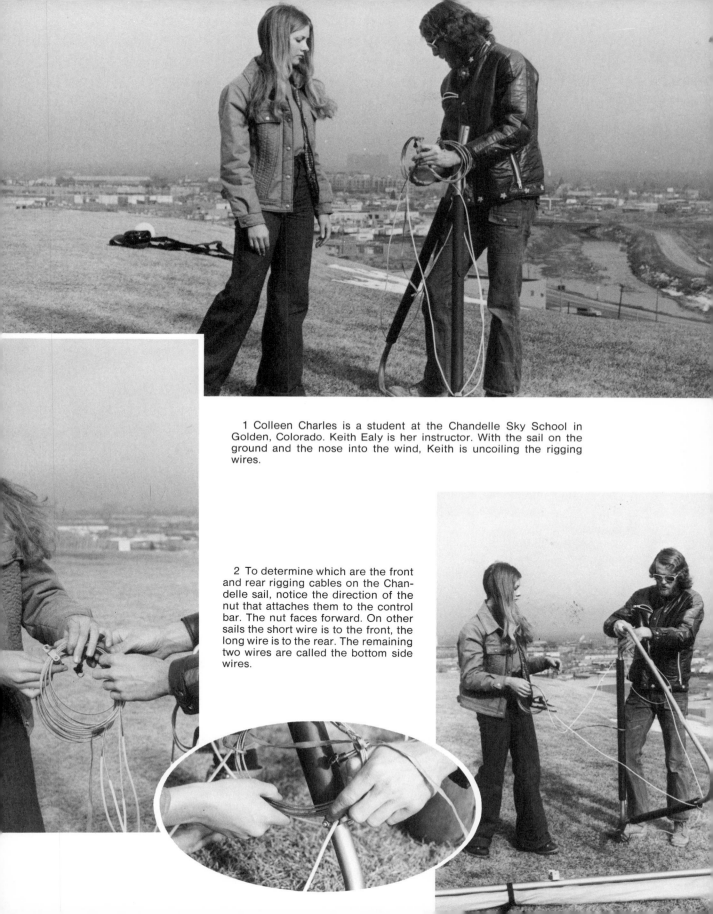

1 Colleen Charles is a student at the Chandelle Sky School in Golden, Colorado. Keith Ealy is her instructor. With the sail on the ground and the nose into the wind, Keith is uncoiling the rigging wires.

2 To determine which are the front and rear rigging cables on the Chandelle sail, notice the direction of the nut that attaches them to the control bar. The nut faces forward. On other sails the short wire is to the front, the long wire is to the rear. The remaining two wires are called the bottom side wires.

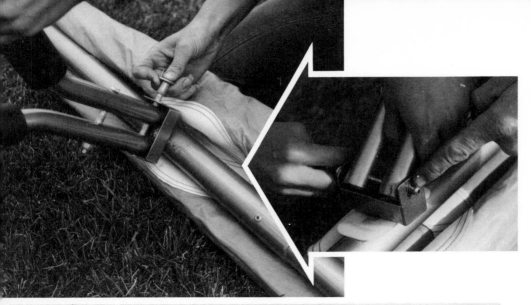

3 Before fastening the rigging wires to the sail, attach the control bar to the control bar box, making certain that the quick-release pin locks in place.

4 Stretch the rigging wires out to the nose of the sail. Be sure there are no twists or kinks.

5 Attach the front wires to the bottom of the nose assembly.
NOTE: The adjustable channel on the nose of this sail is for setting the control bar angle. Check manufacturer's recommendations for proper setting.

6 Lay the sail gently on its side and stretch the wires to the rear, making sure there are no twists or kinks in them.

7 Attach the wires to the tail. Note the adjustment channel; it is designed for "tuning" the sail, adjusting it for differences in control bar angles, harnesses, and special flying conditions.

NOTE: After the control bar and the front and rear wires are attached, it is time to transport the sail to the launching site.

8 Turn the sail over.

9 To pick up the sail, tuck your head under the keel bar so that it rests across your shoulders.

10 This is the most comfortable way to carry the sail.

11 When you reach the launching site, place the nose of the sail into the wind and unfasten the tie-downs. There are usually three or four on a sail. Put the tie-downs in a pocket or in a safe place on your person. After a flight, you'll want to pack up the sail and, if your tie-downs are at the top of the hill, you'll have an irritating hike ahead of you, with a lot of loose sail fabric flapping around.

12 Once you have reached your launch site, swing out the cross bar at right angle to the keel.

13 Be careful not to pinch the sail fabric when you do this.

14 Attach the king post wire on top of the sail to the nose assembly. Make certain that the wire is attached (as illustrated) and securely held in place by the self-locking pip pin.

17 Carefully lay out the bottom control bar side wires. Again, make certain there are no kinks or twists.

18 Bring out the wings by lifting them over the cross bars to avoid damaging the fabric.

15 Lower the tail section and attach the king post wire with turnbuckle assembly to the rear of the keel bar. If you have an assistant, he can help you get the proper tension by gently pulling on the kingpost to create slack in the cable as you tighten the turnbuckle.

16 After you have reached the proper tension, rotate the lock nut down against the turnbuckle assembly, as shown in the next photograph. Check tension in king post wire; it should have 1 inch of play.

NOTE: The tension in the king post wires creates a slight upward curve in the keel bar for proper tuning. This is called the keel tube recurve, and it aids in the proper trimming of the sail.

19 Slide the wing bolt that is attached to the king post side wire through the wing tube and the cross bar. Pick up the bottom side wire and slip over the base of the bolt. Tighten the wing bolt nut to manufacturer's specifications.

20 Tighten the king post side wire turnbuckle until the wire is taut. Rotate the lock nut down against the turnbuckle assembly.

The sail is now assembled.

Preflight Check

YOU might think that the sail is now ready for flight. It has all the outward appearance of being flightworthy, but a person would be foolhardy to take a sail out at this point. There have been numerous reports of pilots who have done this and who have had serious accidents because of a malfunctioning cable, bolt, or turnbuckle. So the next step is an absolute must: it is called the preflight–postassembly checklist, and it should be done before every flight—not just before the first one. The preflight check always begins and ends at the same place.

If you have ever been around aircraft, regardless of their size, you know that the pilot always examines his airplane before take-off. If he doesn't, he is committing an error of omission that could well cause him, his passengers, and the ship itself serious damage. This policy holds for the sky sailor also, and anyone who intends to lift from the ground and sail with the wind must follow his set of preflight rituals in an exacting way.

Under no circumstances should you attempt to fly the sail without first going through the following assembly and preflight check. Although the sail used to demonstrate these procedures is the Chandelle sky sail, the assembly and preflight check are the same for all sails; the differences are in the hardware.

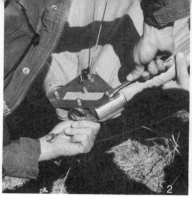

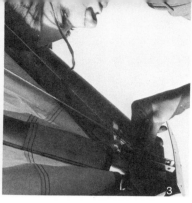

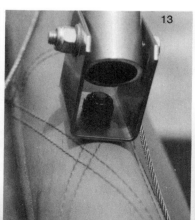

1. Lift nose and examine all nuts and bolts. If all the threads are not above the nut, tighten.

2. Keep a small set of wrenches that fit all the nuts and bolts on the sail with you at all times when flying.

3. Check upper and lower pip pins to insure engaged fit. Be certain lower cables are not twisted.

4. Notice the frayed cable strands showing around the thimble of this clamp. Replace the entire assembly.

5. Look closely for any signs of corrosion on metal parts or bent bolts. Replace if defective.

6. Examine sail-locating screw (holding the sail in place) on wing tube for looseness or fabric damage. Replace if missing —tighten if loose. If sail is torn, repair.

7. Slide hands along both front sides of the wing tubes searching for dents hidden beneath the fabric.

8. If dents are found, examine the wing tube by removing the fabric. A dent like this, although it seems innocent enough, has weakened the tube strength considerably. Don't try to straighten it—replace it.

9. Sight down the left-hand wing tube looking for either right or left warping. If warped, remove tube and have manufacturer straighten.

10. Sight down keel bar tube for straightness and 1–1½" upward recurve in the tail section. If the keel tube does not have this recurve, reset the turnbuckle on the tail of the tube to correct.

11. Sight down right-hand wing tube for straightness and alignment.

12. Slide hands along rear wing tube searching for dents beneath the fabric.

13. Examine nut holding the king post in position. If threads do not extend above the nut, tighten it until they do.

14. Examine the cable attachments at the tail section, making certain all pip-locking pins are firmly seated. Note the perforated channel adjuster here. It provides a safe means of tuning the recurve of the keel tube.

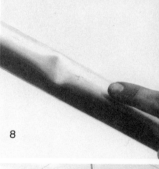

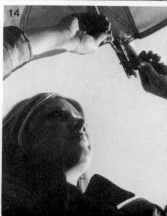

15

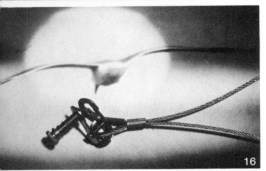

16

17

18

19

15. Observe whether cables are twisted. If so, correct. Look over turnbuckle on top and make certain lock screw is seated down on the top of the turnbuckle. The locating screw that holds the sail fabric in alignment on the keel tube is positioned here. It should be firmly seated and the fabric free of tears.

16. This cable fitting is bent and distorted. Replace it.

17.–18. Scan your eyes over the entire surface of the fabric, carefully looking for tears, holes, rips, stains, or abrasions. If any are discovered, repair.

19. Grasp the keel tube and pull the tail down.

20. Start at the tail of the keel tube and begin feeling the condition of the tube beneath the fabric for dents or tears in fabric.

21. Move on down the keel tube to the nose plate searching for dents and tears.

22. Any dents demand immediate replacement of the entire tube. Do not attempt to straighten; it is worthless. Remove and take it to the nearest recycling depot so the aluminum can have a new life as a beer can or Venetian blind.

23. Check the control bar bracket around bolt head and be certain the box has no play. Pip pin balls should be completely through the control bar bracket. Check for dents or kinks in the cross bar. Examine the harness bolt for bends and control bar cracks or signs of weakness at the harness bolt holes.

24. If the control bar locking pin is bent, replace it. Some turnbuckles of the type shown here, although airworthy, have one disadvantage: unless they are wire-locked when adjusted through the locking holes in the turnbuckle body, its impossible to tell how many threads of the eye strap bolt penetrate down into the bolt's center section. The bolt could have one thread engaged or several; there is no way of knowing. It is recommended to use hardware that can be checked by eye and touch. Never use standard hardware items. Use only standard aircraft hardware.

20

21

22

23

24

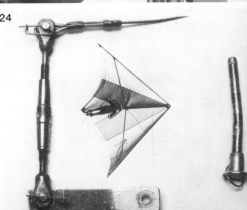

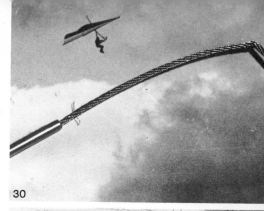

25. Snap open and close the harness caribiner to make certain it is not bent or jammed. The caribiner should open and close to the rear of the control bar—one pilot had his open to the front and, when he took off on a launch, the harness strap popped out and he had to really white knuckle it and hang on until he landed.

26. Examine the control bar cable shackles on both sides. The nuts holding them to the control bar should face toward the nose of the sail.

27. All the cables should be free of frays, kinks, or bends. If they are not, replace.

NOTE: A complete set of replacement cables cost about $20–30. If there's any doubt about the condition of them, replace.

28. The shank balls are swaged at the factory with a special machine and are tested to hold beyond the breaking tension of the cable–about 1000 lbs tension. The manufacturer leaves a small portion of the cable exposed on the end of the ball. If for any reason this small portion of cable is absent, replace the cable immediately. The cable could fail. Notice the missing protruding wires on the ball on the right.

29. Examine the eye strap lock ring, making certain it is securely in place.

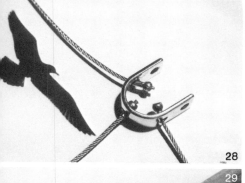

30. If the eye strap is bent, reject. If any wire on the sky sail is as bent as this one, its strength is reduced by fifty percent. The cable will break at this kink even if it is straightened.

31. Check the wing bolts and palm grip nuts to see that they are tight and secure.

32. All the bolts should be straight and free of bends. After a hard landing they may bend, as the wing bolt on the left illustrates. Do not attempt to straighten. Further bending will only weaken it. Replace it.

33. Check tension on the king post cables (1–1½" play) and turnbuckle adjustment.

34. Make certain the safety ring is in place on the turnbuckle thread.

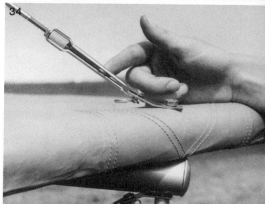

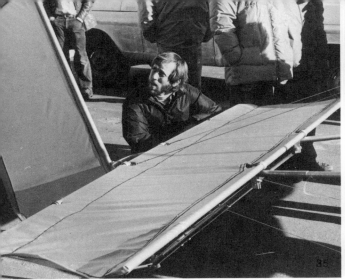

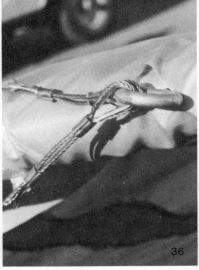

35. Gordy Cummings of Golden Colarado (one of the Sky Sailing Engineers of Chandelle and an accomplished flyer) examines the tail assembly of a *Quicksilver* monoplane to make certain that the assembly is airworthy.

36. For those sails that use the nico press cable retainers. Check each of the clamps for possible wear, broken cable strands, and signs of damage in the eye or thimble of the cable (the loop that secures the cable to the eyebolt). Pay particular attention to the king post assembly, going over every detail with the scrutiny of a tax collector. Remember, once in the air, it is impossible to repair any of those clamps or retainers if they break or come loose. Use only nico press tools for repairs.

Care and Cleaning of the Sky Sail

Check the entire surface of the sail for holes, tears, and any foreign materials such as mildew, rust, water, oil stains, and battery acid.

When stains are discovered, they should be removed at once, not for cosmetic appearances but for their threat to safety, and steps must be taken to detect, neutralize, and correct the trouble before deterioration really starts.

Look for areas which may have come in contact with harmful foreign substances, such as acid, oil, or salt water. Stains brought on by milder substances are a common indicator of deterioration. Stains generally appear as a discoloration or blemish in the material, usually distinguished by a circular ring. Salt water stains are characterized by the appearance of a white crystalline substance on the surface. Oil stains are recognizable by their brown-to-black color and the oily feeling when rubbed between the fingers. Acid stains on white material appear as a grayish, powdery ash. On darker materials, acid stains tend to bleach. Acid causes rapid deterioration on all materials.

Rust, mildew, and acid stains will spread throughout the sail unless checked immediately; therefore, they must be neutralized or cut out entirely. Mildew is removed by washing with a mild soap or liquid detergent. Mildew has little effect on dacron and will not form unless some other feeding media are present. Rust stains cannot be neutralized or removed with approved cleaning agents. They must be cut out to at least ½″ beyond the stained area. Regions deteriorated by acid must be cut out to 1 inch beyond the affected area; but if the area is greater than 8 square inches, the entire section must be replaced. Stains not recognizable should be noted and the sail returned to the manufacturer.

Those stains which are considered harmful because of their visible effects to the material should be patched. Most grease and oil stains can be wholly or partially removed by applying the proper cleaning solvent—trichlor-ethylene or methyl-ethyl-ketone. (Warning: These are highly toxic and flammable.)

Excerpted from U.S. Navy training manual NAVPERS 10358-D.

37. Wherever you are, regardless of the crowds or weather, examine every part of your sail before you fly and immediately after landing for possible damage to the sail. Here is Bob Wills going through his check list after one of his many flights in California.

37

This preflight check we have just conducted should be repeated before each flight. To neglect doing so can result in a failure in any of the areas we have just covered. Even if you should use someone else's sky sail for a flight, never take the owner's word for the condition of his sail. The responsibility of determining the flying ability of the sky sail is yours alone. Remember, your life depends on it.

Good flying sites are not always safe flying sites when an emergency landing is imminent. Rocks and boulders cannot always be avoided. The pilot should always assume that his flying site will be strewn with obstacles and take along adequate protective clothing—including helmet; sturdy clothes; elbow, knee, and shin protectors; and heavy shoes or boots.

Preflight Protective Clothing

Flying above trees and ground skimming on sandy beaches present a new set of problems. Nose-in landings on sand can produce some bad cases of elbow, shin, knee, and chin rash. Trees, when you happen to land in one, can poke branches into your body in the most unwelcome places. Always wear a helmet, and when flying over trees the helmet should have a face protector. Don't forget heavy duty clothing, gloves, and knee and shin protectors.

Phyllis Somer of Beverly Hills is an example of a Californian's fearless attitude toward sky sailing. She presided as Queen of the Annie Green Springs National Hang-Gliding Championships in Sylmar, California. Her costume is visually attractive but immensely impractical for any flyer to emulate. Here she's going through one of the basic ground handling maneuvers.

ANY sport that involves motion can cause damage to our bodies. The severity of the injuries inflicted depends on a number of factors, many of which we can anticipate. But there are other dangerous areas that only an experienced flier would know about. We are now going to explore those areas.

Since the sport of sky sailing is so new, a comprehensive set of safety rules for flying has as yet not been devised. There are six basic areas where strict safety rules should apply. They are:

- The aircraft
- Clothing and harness
- Launch sites
- Weather conditions
- Flying right of ways
- First aid

Let's take them one at a time: we have covered the safe sky sail; now let's look at the pilot's protective clothing, his harness, and basic first aid.

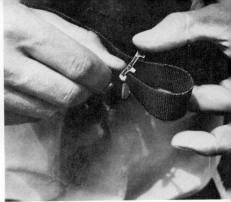

The first aid requirements for first flights usually are little more than bruised elbows or knees, so a sturdy jacket is helpful. Here Colleen is putting on padded knee protectors of a type that are inexpensive and can be purchased at any sporting goods store. They are important because on many of the first flights the pilot lands on his knees before his feet. The hiking boots are ideal. They support the ankles and have good grip soles.

Put on the harness. Colleen has chosen the seated harness to start with because of the terrain. Two straps go over the shoulders and one around the chest. It takes a little time to get used to the straps.

Make certain you thread the fastener properly for a secure fit.

The wide seat goes to the rear under your buttocks and is held on by smaller leg straps.

A helmet is a must. This one is a Bell model made especially for sky sailing. It allows wind to get underneath: thus, the pilot can "hear the wind" so he can estimate his speed when flying. Other helmets, like the motorcycle styles have also have been used. Whatever you use, make certain it fits well and doesn't slide around on your head. Avoid those with chin cups. They can slip off on a hard impact right at the moment the helmet is most needed.

Sturdy gloves should be worn at all time when you fly, not for protection from th wind and weather, but for that mome you contact the ground. Gloves will pr tect the hands and knuckles from bruis if the flyer should land while still hangin onto the control bar. Skiing or motorc cle gloves with padding over the knuc les are the best.

Ground Handling PART 1

This ground handling practice can be done in any area large enough to set up and maneuver the sail, such as a back yard or a parking lot. Wind is not necessary, as you are merely familiarizing yourself with the sail.

In the following basic moves do not attach the harness to the sail, even though you are wearing it. This is a safety precaution to prevent an accident in the event a gust of wind should blow over the sail. It is recommended that every beginner spend a great deal of time in ground-handling practice. This effort will help him overcome the awkwardness and weight of the sail.

Take your kite to a convenient, clear, open space on a day when there is a fair breeze of 5 to 7 miles, so that you can get a feel of the sail in the wind. After you have practiced a few times, take the sail out on a windy day (10–20 mph) and you will discover the full potential of the sail. If the wind should toss the sail around, let it go. No harm will come to it. But under no circumstances should you hook up the harness to the sail at this stage of your training.

1. There are two basic methods of holding the control bar. The method shown here is one of them; as we progress we will illustrate the other. With the nose into the wind, place the right foot over the bottom of the control bar and grasp the sides of the control bar as Colleen here demonstrates. It is best to perform these basic steps on a gentle, breezy day only.

2. Rotate the nose of the sail up and straight and level into the wind and remove the foot from the control bar. The streamer hanging from the front rigging cables is there to assist in keeping the nose of the sail into the wind.

3. Lift the sail up and place it on the top of your right foot and get a comfortable hold on the control bar (with one hand at the lower junction where the side meets the bottom of the control bar and the other hand above the cable shackle).

4. Stand up keeping the sail level into the wind and held at the belt line. At this point, you stay in this position until you feel comfortable with the sail. The wind will start to play with the sail, and the student will have a little difficulty keeping the sail level and into the wind. While going through this maneuver you will discover which method of holding the sail is the most comfortable.

5. Here Colleen, a small woman, found the first method of holding the sail awkward, so she shifted to the more comfortable both-hands-on-the-bar method. Either way is acceptable. Practice this procedure until you feel comfortable and can control the sail in this first position without the wind getting underneath the sail and pitching it around.

6. Now that you've got the sail und control, we make the first move. Alwa keep the nose level and into the wi and move the control bar to the right. flight this is the movement that will i tiate a left-hand turn. Be certain to ke the bottom of the control bar at wa level.

10. The wind will get under the sail and the fabric will bloom upwards, making the sail difficult to handle. When this happens, stop your forward motion and bring the control bar back to your waist.

11. Put the sail back on the ground and start to bring the nose back down into the wind by *pulling* the control bar back to the waist. The position of the elbows is important here. Notice their position in frame 10. The elbows are behind the control bar. In this position they will keep the sail from pitching back over the shoulders.

12. Rotate the nose back down to th ground (as in picture 1) and into th wind, and you have completed the fir basic moves that should be mastered b fore moving on to the next step.

7. Next, swing the control bar to the left. This movement in the air will initiate a right-hand turn. Repeat all these movements until you can do them comfortably while keeping the nose into the wind and the sail level.

8. Moving forward with the sail is a little more difficult, as the nose has a tendency to raise when you step forward. It is vital that you learn how to move forward while keeping the sail level and pointing into the wind. Practice this movement until you can master it. Here Colleen is having a little difficulty keeping the nose down. Practice, practice, practice!

9. Once moving forward with the sail level and heading into the wind is mastered, we now move to the flare. In flight, this movement, when modified, is used to climb at launch and to stop moving forward when landing. While moving with the sail level and the control bar at waist level, *push* forward on the bar, raising the nose into the wind.

Taking Down the Sky Sail

Here Don Beuch of Chandelle demonstrates one of the recommended procedures for dismantling a sky sail: After each day's flight, the sky sail must be taken down and packed away for transporting and for later storage in the garage or home. This procedure should be as exacting as the assembly. Whatever method the manufacturer recommends or your flight instructor suggests should be carefully followed. Otherwise, the fabric may be torn; wires bent, kinked or damaged; retaining pins lost; or tubes bent.

Release the king post support cables. Retract the wing tubes to the keel bar. Rotate the cross tube, align it with keel, and lower the king post to its nesting place between the wing tubes.

Taking Down the Sky Sail

1. Lift the left-hand sail, shake out all the wrinkles, and hold it in the same position as shown.

2. Fold over the top leading edge of the sail, keeping all edges taut.

3. Place the edge down next to the keel bar.

4. Roll the outside edge into a tightly aligned (all the way to the nose) roll.

5. Make certain during this procedure not to allow any creases or folds to get into the roll as you move on down to the center of the sail.

6. When you reach the center, tuck the roll between the left-hand wing tube and the keel bar to prevent the roll from unwinding.

7. Smooth out the edge before starting to roll it up.

8. Tuck it between the right-hand wing tube and the keel bar.

9. Roll up the king post wires and tuck them into the center fold.

10. Adjust the wing fabric over the king post cables so they are securely tucked in.

11. Remove the sail retaining straps that you placed in your pocket during the sail assembly lesson. You should have at least three of them.

12. Tie up the sail with the straps and remove the control bar.

13. Remember how you attached the control bar in lesson one! When you remove the locking pin, insert it back into the control box and be sure the pin-locking mechanism is engaged. If you lose it in transport, days of sailing will be lost while you are waiting to get another. If the pin does not have a restraining attachment, some flyers attach it to the control box with a strong rubber band or twine looped through the wire ring on the head of the pin.

14. Roll up the fore and aft control cables and lock them into the caribiner.

15. Slide the sail protective covering over the sail and secure the end. The sail is now protected from the wind and elements.

NOTE: During this breakdown procedure, inspect the sail carefully for rips and tears and repair them immediately. If the sail is wet, allow it to dry before storing for any length of time.

Transporting the Sky Sail

The sky sail is tough, but it becomes vulnerable when it's not in the air. The tubes can get bent and the fabric ripped or damaged if it is not securely fastened to the top of the car. A rack (the ski rack type) can be used as a base to keep the sail from rocking back and forth. It should be firmly tied down. A sky sail flying off the top of the car is potentially a dangerous piece of equipment.

1. Here is one method of transporting sky sails on a truck. Special brackets were built to securely hold several sails.

2. Here Chris Wills is shown tying down his sail so it won't rattle or chafe while the truck is bouncing around on rough roads.

3. If a car is used, make certain the front and tail sections are securely tied down so that it is impossible for the sail to swing left or right while driving. Here the owner of the sky sail has left the control bar attached.

4. Attach a red streamer at the tail. Check your local highway department regulations for details on marking the tail of the sail.

NOTE: If you travel by air, check with your airline agent about accompanying sports equipment. Many have reduced rates.

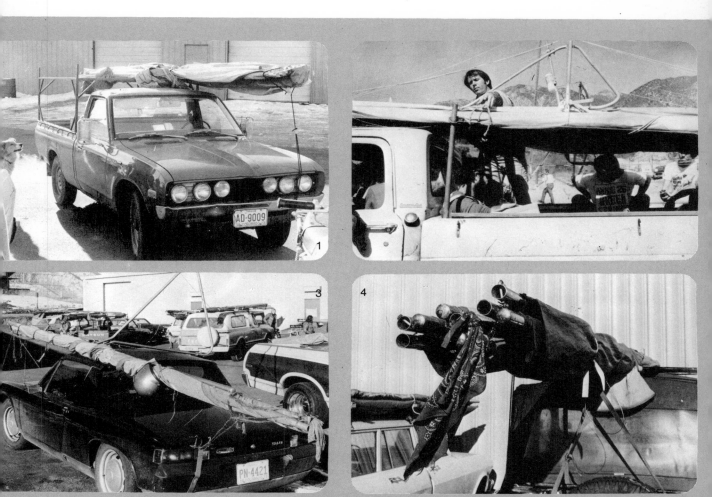

Ground Handling

PART 2

In this next series of training exercises, the pilot is going to discover how the sail handles while in motion. This is one of the most important training procedures. It is here the pilot will discover the potential of the sail, its personality, flying capabilities and its quirks.

During these exercises the pilot should suit up with all the protective clothing specified. He should wear a harness, if he owns one, during these exercises, so that he will become accustomed to the feel of it. It is not essential, however, to wear a harness for these exercises. It is important to be patient. It takes a bird more than a day to learn to fly. So it is with the fledgling pilot. The following is a check list that should be followed before each flight.

Things to remember before leaving for the flying area-
Checklist:
1. The complete sky sail. All parts plus a set of wrenches that fit all the nuts and bolts. The forward (or front) cables should have a plastic coating, either as standard equipment, or the owner of the sail can purchase plastic sleeves from a marine supplier and install them himself. They prevent cable burns if you should hit one on a hard landing. A roll of good, strong sail repair tape to repair the sail if it should get torn during the exercise should be included. So should a Dwyer wind meter (which costs about $5 from most sky sail manufacturers) which will be needed to test the wind.

2. Protective Clothing:
   A flying helmet that fits well.
   A sturdy jacket or heavy sweater and a pair of heavy-duty pants or slacks for the women—no skirts or thin slacks.
   Strong gloves with knuckle protectors or padding.
   A pair of sturdy boots, high enough to support the ankles. The hiking types that can be seen in many of the pictures here are excellent.
   Knee and shin protectors (children's hockey or baseball knee and shin protectors are the ones shown here)—they are inexpensive and can be purchased at any sporting goods store.

3. A simple, compact first aid kit should be taken on all flights. It should include antiseptics, bandages and Band-Aids, cotton, tape, small scissors, merthiolate or Mercurochrome, and the name of your doctor if you have any kind of medical disability.

4. When selecting a flying area, look for a gentle slope (12°–20°) with the wind no more than 10 mph (Dwyer wind meter) blowing up its slope (golf courses, parks, or countrysides). It is wise to ask permission to use these sites, for in most cases the owners or park officials will be grateful that you asked. Be considerate of the property you use. Do not litter; rather, clean up the area before you leave, and your chances of being welcomed back will be greatly enhanced.

5. The Buddy System: When flying or practicing you should have fellow fliers or friends around to act as observers. They can comment on your exercises and help you correct any mistakes or difficulties with technique. It is helpful to have someone take notes or Super 8 movies of your exercises and subsequent flights (it is a practical use for the movie camera). Not only are such films a record of each of your flights, but, when viewed later on, they will serve as an excellent teaching tool for you and your friends.

It is also suggested that you start keeping a log book—a procedure recommended by the United States Hang Gliding Association for several reasons. It not only serves as a detailed account of your progress, but will be a permanent record of all your flights for possible use later on. Your log should contain the flier and/or fliers' name(s), date, time, place, wind and weather conditions, date of purchase and type of sail flown, condition of sail-rigging, and number of flights flown with your sail. Also, anyone who flies your kite, including yourself should note his weight and experience. Each successful flight should be recorded with estimated or precise flight times. All hard landings or crashes and comments on how the crash occurred should be noted. All injuries should be included, as should treatments for the injuries. All pre-flight observations of damage to sail and, if replacement parts are used, the date, manufacture, name, and reason for replacement should be included in the log.

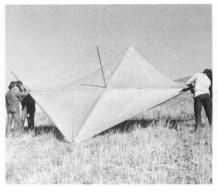

At the chosen flying site, carry your sails in a manner illustrated here. Some fliers prefer to attach the control bar first. If you do, always hook up the front and rear wires; otherwise the control bar, not being supported by the cables, could damage the control bar box on the keel.

Find a gentle slope no more than 20° and set up the sail, nose into the wind. Preflight check before proceeding.

Rotate the nose up into the wind. When all is ready, examine the field in front for rocks, posts, pot holes, or other obstructions, and move them or yourself to a location free of anything that you might trip or stumble over.

NOTE: If the training field is nothing more than soft grass or sand, the shin and knee protectors are not absolutely necessary because the pilot is not harnessed or hooked up to the sail. So if the sail should get away from the student, he need only let loose to avoid a spill. It is my own personal opinion that protective clothing should be worn at all times.

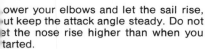

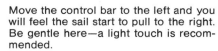

Raise the sail. Locate the control bar at the waist line and repeat the left and right movements of the control bar as practiced in Lesson One.

Lower your elbows and let the sail rise, but keep the attack angle steady. Do not let the nose rise higher than when you started.

Raise the nose up slightly and feel the pressure of the wind. This movement tells you how strong the wind is, so you can angle the sail properly.

Move the control bar to the left and you will feel the sail start to pull to the right. Be gentle here—a light touch is recommended.

Start to move slowly at first and you will feel the sails billow up, and the fabric will tighten causing the control bar to tug up.

Now move the control bar to the right and the sail will pull to the left. Don't force these movements. It should all happen gently and easily.

Slow down and stop. Place the control bar on the ground and lower the nose into the wind. Move around to the front of the control bar and pick up the sail (nose down and into the wind) and walk back to the starting point. Be careful when stepping over the front control cables so as not to damage them.

Now let's see the same thing over again, but this time the take-off is a fast one, which, if done on a good slope, would commit the sail to flight. The take-off is strong—no pussyfooting. Elbows up and against the control bar. Head forward—toes dig in.

Flare. The sail blooms up and lifts. Elbows down. Nose angle—perfect. Feet still pounding.

Turn to the left. Push bar to the right and the sail will guide you right along with it in a gentle arc.

Slowly, gently slide the control bar to the left and the sail will bank to the right. Feet—still going.

Pow! The sail wants to fly—its lift is so strong it will haul you off the ground. Let go and let the sail land on its own.

That looked easy enough. The fliers demonstrating this basic technique are experienced pilots. Now let's examine what can happen when the student pilot tries it.

"Man does not need an engine to fly, not even for launching, and we come closer to pure human flight by severing ourselves from the infernal combustion engine and all its problems."

W. A. Allen *(from* Ground Skimmer, *No. 4, August 1972)*

MISTAKES

THE TIMID TAKEOFF
is the most common error the student pilot makes. In addition, he pushed out before he had enough forward thrust and neglected to lower his elbows.

These errors must be corrected before attempting your first flight.

NO SPEED, NO LIFT
It is important to begin on a fast run. He didn't. The nose is too high, his elbows should be down. Remember: start fast!

The take-off should be fast and steady, with the nose angle slightly raised.

The sail starts into a left-hand turn without proper pilot control. Arms not down. Out of control.

Left-wing tip digs into the turf and starts to flip over. Pilot should release the sail at this point and let it go.

Nose too high, elbows not down, and left wing dipping.

Nose too high: attack angle dangerously increasing. To correct, lower elbows and pull control bar back to bring the nose down.

Nose too low: unsteady run, and the wing tip makes contact with the earth and starts down.

When the nose goes down during a run, stop all forward movement and begin the run again. The student in this photo did not, and here's what happens.

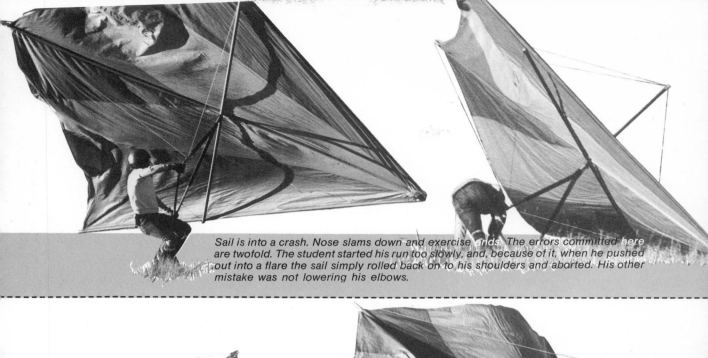

Sail is into a crash. Nose slams down and exercise ends. The errors committed here are twofold. The student started his run too slowly, and, because of it, when he pushed out into a flare the sail simply rolled back on to his shoulders and aborted. His other mistake was not lowering his elbows.

Holding on to the sail in a crash situation can hurt both the pilot and the sail. Release it when you sense the sail is about to flip over.

Out of control. Wing dramatically yaws to the left and contacts the ground. To correct at this point, pull nose down and level the sail.

The pilot tried to correct the wing tip contact by using brute force to bring the nose down, instead of allowing the wind to assist him. The nose kept on going, slamming itself and the pilot into the earth.

"The biggest obstacle at the beginning is how to hold the kite on the ground. Once you're in the air it's easy . . . in the air you're concentrating on your glide path. The first time I flew I felt really natural . . . it's really simple."
Cindy Hayden (Sylmar)

Crash. . . . The pilot and the sail make a thumping nose-in.

Practice again and again and again until these exercises are performed with skill and ease.

First Flight
"B" LEVEL 1

HAVING practiced the flying movements to perfection on the ground, we now move forward to the first flight. It will be an experience you will long remember, so have your friend with a movie or still camera ready for the event.

The procedure for this exercise is exactly the same as it was for ground handling the sail, only now we will hook up the harness. If you have mastered all the problems of basic flight on the ground, this phase of your training should be the most fun. It is here that the thrilling experience of personal flight is enjoyed without the aid of any power other than that of the wind, your sail, and yourself.

Solving the Fear Syndrome

It helps to realize that the fear of heights shared by most people is not the fear of heights per se, but is actually the fear of falling from them . . . especially from a precipitous place come upon suddenly. The emotion is not related to the actual height either. Any fear you may have is based on a lack of confidence in your ability to fly safely back down. The fear syndrome is handled by a combination of common sense and self-awareness; common sense to avoid potentially dangerous flying situations, and self-awareness to know your flying capabilities and stay within your limits. It's that simple. Work your way up gradually. There is an old saying: there are old pilots and there are bold pilots, but there are no pilots who are both old and bold.

Kent Trimble
Manta Products

Before You Fly

THERE ARE BASIC RULES YOU SHOULD FOLLOW AND ENCOURAGE OTHERS TO IF THEY ARE NEW TO THE SPORT. THESE RULES SHOULD BE SCRUPULOUSLY ADHERED TO:

1. Preflight check your sail before each flight, and keep the nose into the wind.

2. Make certain you are wearing all your protective clothing and that your harness fits properly.

3. For these exercises pick a shallow slope. It will keep you from getting too high too soon.

4. Allow no show-offs or fooling around. Flying is a serious business. You and all your friends and fellow fliers are ambassadors for the sport. Observers will judge you by your conduct, and this includes no littering of the area. Leave nature as it was before you arrived.

5. Check the wind direction and speed. The wind should not exceed 10 mph for this exercise. The wind should be fairly consistent as it blows up the hill. Do not attempt to fly if the wind is gusty or if it shifts direction quickly —it could cause a bad crash. Instead, pack up your sail and go home. Your chances of flying another day will be enhanced by this wise decision, as most serious accidents are caused by shifty, gusty winds.

6. Examine the take-off and landing area carefully for obstructions that can cause injury to the sail and yourself.

7. Preflight the flying area by running with the sail before you hook up the harness, as winds generally decrease as you near the bottom of a hill.

8. Control movements should be slow and easy at all times. Flying is a gentle, subtle sport. There is no room for foolishness here.

9. Never overestimate your skill or be drawn into flying above your talents. As you progress you will acquire new skills in handling the sail. Be sure not to rush yourself. Take your time as you learn, and you will have many exciting flights without injury.

10. Have a first aid kit handy. If anyone is seriously injured, do not move him. Call professional help.

11. After a hard landing or crash, examine the sail carefully. Give broken or damaged parts immediate attention. Repair the sail immediately or do not use it again until it has been repaired. If you are unable or confused about how to repair your sail, ask an expert.

12. If you should crash, find out why, so you can avoid another such mistake. Finally, duly note all events of the day in the log book.

NEVER FLY ALONE

First Flight

Note: All these photographs of students enjoying their first flights were taken at the Chandelle Sky School, Colorado.

When the harness is attached to the sail, the chest strap should be level with the control bar. If it is too high or too low the sail becomes difficult to handle.

Take a trial run down the hill, without attaching the harness, to check the wind, the sail, and the terrain.

Lay down the shoe leather hard. Keep the nose attack angle constant. Keep moving. Take one or two additional steps after you think you are about to lift off.

Suddenly you find that you are airborne. Do not anticipate this lift off by jumping into the air. Keep your feet going until there is nothing for them to dig into.

Here is another example of a successful first flight. The student starts a 'hot' run down the slope. Sail is level with the horizon or the wind, not with the slope.

He feels the lift as his harness straps tighten, and then he pushes out the control bar and is up in the air. Look for your landing area and start to flare.

With the nose heading into the wind, grasp the control bar and lift the sail up and start your run.

Lift the sail until the harness strap is tight and you can lift the sail no higher. Move out fast, angling the nose up slightly.

Tuck up your feet and keep the nose angle up, but do not push it out any further.

Anticipate your landing. Lower your feet and start to push on the control bar to raise the nose into a flare. Always unhook the harness after every landing.

He holds the sail in the flare position and prepares to land.

With the sail flared, all forward movement will stop and you touch down at zero speed.

MISTAKES

The most frequent error is not the fear of flying but the lack of sufficient speed or commitment on the run before lift off, complicated by over-reaction to the controls once in the air. Practice these take-offs and landings until you can do them with skill and ease. Don't think for a moment that this stage of your flight training will be drudgery. As you get better and better your flight duration will increase. Flights of one to two minutes at heights of 10 to 20 feet can be achieved on these "ground skimming" exercises. Your flying knowledge will increase as each flight is logged. A word of caution: The student pilot should never attempt to fly at greater altitudes until the straight forward flight is mastered.

His forward direction has ceased. He is dropping back to earth.

The student pilot pushed the control bar out into a flare before he had sufficient air speed and is heading for a stall.

The tail of the sail digs into the turf, leaving the startled pilot hanging.

NOTE: Preflight the sail carefully after crashes, particularly the tail and nose sections.

With the sail stalled, the nose tips and plows into the grass. The remedy is more ground speed before pushing out the control bar for take-off.

When the student is timid in his take-off run he winds up at the bottom of the hill, totally winded. When he starts back up the hill, that 35-pound sail feels like a ton. The solution is to get moving on take-off.

Run too slow . . . nose drooping . . . elbows not down . . . right wing going down.

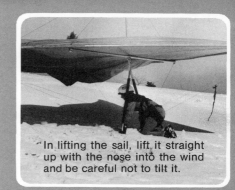

In lifting the sail, lift it straight up with the nose into the wind and be careful not to tilt it.

Lost air speed . . . sail collapses . . . pilot trips . . . and tries to correct run.

Nose up . . . wind gets under the left wing and moves it upward with considerable force.

Wind gets under left wing and lifts and . . .

Nose going higher. The correct procedure here would be to get the nose down into the wind.

Rams the nose into the ground. Remedy—fast, steady run and holding the sail into the wind until flaring.

Over she goes. Try again. Remember: always unhook the harness the moment you complete your flight. As you can see, if Colleen hadn't she would have been in trouble here.

PRACTICE

First Flight

A good start for Colleen . . . elbows up; pull up on sail until tension is felt on harness suspension line. Keep the sail level with the nose heading into the wind. Continue running down the hill until the sail fills with air and . . .

lifts you off the ground. Drop elbows and push out on the control bar, lifting the nose into a perfect angle of attack. Lift your feet and you're airborne.

Still gaining altitude, but watch out: the nose is moving away from a direct wind heading, and the left wing is lifting. Keep the streamer on the front rigging wire pointing straight at you, and bring the nose back into the wind.

Good body and feet position. She's flying into the wind now. Do not move the control bar. Keep it steady and fly straight into the wind.

To land, gently push the control bar out so that the sail will flare. The feet should be together and pointing straight down under the control bar.

Instead of making a perfect, two-feet-on-the-ground landing, Colleen swung her feet forward. Her natural instinct was to pull the control bar back to get her feet under her again, but this action pulled the nose down.

A split second later the forward thrust of the sail rolled Colleen out from under the control bar, but because she was in ground contact she was dragged forward until all motion stopped . . . a typical ending for a first flight.

*"I flew.
I really flew.
I want to do it again."*

VENTURE THY FATE SKYWARD
TO FEEL WHAT FEELS THE BIRD
THE GRASP OF SUN
AND EARTH
THE JOY OF FEATHERED
BIRD. . . .

The Hominid Avian

"Flying really goes in stages; you can see it with everybody. When you first start to fly it's "How high am I," and you made it 60 feet and you made it 100 feet and then you get out of the height idea and you get into the performance of the sail, and then you want to get distance, and then you want to get time and distance, and then you get into the maneuvers. Just the other day I made my first turn and it was the most incredible sensation because by turning you feel more a part of the kite . . . everything because you can feel it from your toes to your head . . . when your feet are hanging you really feel like a bird. You feel the wind on you and the flutter of the sail. It really is like you're a part of it. It becomes more so when you start working it and you feel you're not controlling it and it's not controlling you; you're working together as a team—just up there flying.

"You look at a bird fly and everything is precision, it's very natural. In flying, to get that same precision down, that's the challenge for me."

Karen Rowley

Wind Direction and Speed

THE air the sky sail flies in is as important to the pilot as the air he breathes. It is a life and death concern. The most common cause of sky sailing accidents is a lack of understanding of the behavior of the air. So the student pilot must make every effort to learn as much as possible about the wind and air. He can acquire this knowledge in several ways: by personal experience, through discussions with fellow fliers, and by reading about the sport in magazines that specialize in sky sailing. Here we can offer the basics.

There are two types of wind or air: stable and unstable. Stable air or wind blows in a horizontal plane. Unstable air is caused when updrafts, downdrafts, or thermals, break through the horizontal flow and create turbulence. Both types require special flying tactics.

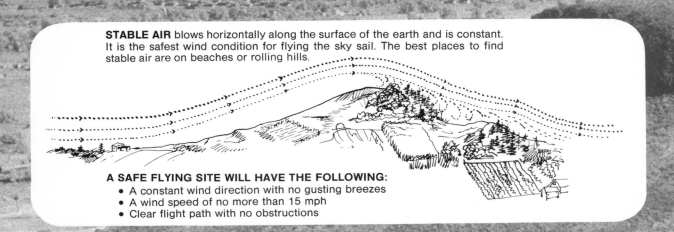

STABLE AIR blows horizontally along the surface of the earth and is constant. It is the safest wind condition for flying the sky sail. The best places to find stable air are on beaches or rolling hills.

A SAFE FLYING SITE WILL HAVE THE FOLLOWING:
- A constant wind direction with no gusting breezes
- A wind speed of no more than 15 mph
- Clear flight path with no obstructions

UNSTABLE AIR: When stable air comes in contact with an obstruction, such as mountains, cliffs, trees, buildings, or a strong thermal updraft, it becomes unstable as it forms turbulent air pockets around the obstacle. These conditions make flying extremely hazardous for the novice.

Study this drawing carefully and notice how the air forms a variety of air currents: downdrafts, updrafts or thermals, and rotors that curl backwards from the main wind line thrust. A flight path from the top of the hill to any spot below is full of potential flying hazards. Air is invisible so the pilot should know how the air reacts when it contacts an obstacle.

- Thermals are created when air currents are forced upwards from dry heated surfaces of the earth.
- Rotors are formed when the wind strikes a sheer cliff face, sand dune, or mountainside and boils over the top edge.
- Downdrafts are formed on the lee side of buildings, trees, ravines, gullies, or other obstacles that deviate from the flat earth surface.

A sky sail flying into any of these air currents is forced into a flight path that coincides with the direction of the air. Unless the flier has developed enough flying experience to enable him to fly out of these hazards, he is in for some very hard landings.

"I feel like I'm almost in a no-man's land; like I'm not really supposed to be there. You're out in the open with nothing around you; sometimes you forget you even have a kite. You see many things; deer and of course all the soaring birds, you notice birds in the air all the time. We have literally learned to soar from the birds. They are the masters and we just follow them. Most of the small birds get out of the way, and the big hawks come over to look at you. Oftentimes they'll just cruise up alongside and look at you a while and you look at them. You know that he's got his wings tucked way in, running about one tenth of his efficiency, and you're flat out with all your efficiency and you get a little annoyed after a while, so you'll yell at him or something and generally they'll peel off and really show you how to fly."

Dave Kilbourne

1. Wind Over Obstacles: Obstacles such as trees, barns, and houses disrupt the air flow and cause different patterns in the lee (or back) side of these obstacles. If you should fly into one of these downdrafts, the sail would sink and crash into the obstacle, so fly well above them.

2. Avoiding Obstacles: To gain air speed is essential, so pull in the control bar and dive towards the obstacles. When the sail gains sufficient air speed, push into a flare, sail over the obstacles, and look for a clear landing area.

5. Gusty, High, or Cross Winds: Winds ranging from 25 to 45 mph are killer winds. Any pilot flying in such winds is risking his life or at least considerable damage to his sail. This type of wind is by far the worst enemy of sky sailing and should be consistently avoided.

6. Wind Loss: Flying off a high ridge and down into a canyon can mean the end of the flight, as wind usually dies down completely here even though it is blowing steadily all around the valley. A take-off in such an area usually means a premature landing.

9. Ridge Soaring: The strongest lift is in front and above the crest of the ridge. To either side the wind will drop off and lose all upward thrust. Flying too close to the face of the ridge can result in a crash because of the turbulence created by the rising wind buffeting the face.

10. Dune Soaring: Ocean winds are the most constant and provide excellent wind for soaring. The take-off point on the top of the dunes positions the glider in a perfect nose into the wind heading. The sandy beaches are excellent landing areas.

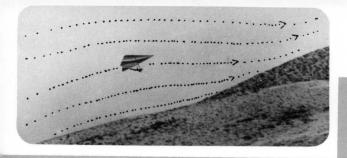

3. Wind blows in many directions over fixed objects. When flying in hilly areas, be aware of these directions. If a turn is committed too soon after launch, the sail can easily be sucked around the edge and into the side of the hill or obstacle, and a serious crash can result. This type of wind-direction change is perhaps one of the most dangerous hazards of sky sailing.

4. Downwind Launch: Downwind launches are extremely hazardous and should never be attempted. The force of the wind will be pressing on top of the sail, and chances are the flight will end up on the side of the mountain, as air speed for good lift will be virtually impossible.

7. Thermals or Updrafts: Thermals are present on clear, calm days and are the result of warm air rising up to the base of clouds. Thermals are usually the domain of hawks and sailplanes, but more and more Rogallo flyers are flying these exciting winds.

8. Heavy Trees: Flying between trees at ski resorts requires considerable flying skill. The wind moving up the slope shifts as the slope curves. If the sail should fly over the trees, there could be a serious wind loss because the air rising off the cleared slope would be absorbed by the trees.

Rules to Follow

- Always take off and land into the wind.
- Wind usually decreases from the top to the bottom of a hill and can be blowing in a different direction.
- The depth of turbulence depends on the wind force creating it.
- Ridge soaring is cross wind flying. Nose angle should always be into the wind to keep from being blown into the ridge.
- All turns should be made away from the ridge.
- Wind velocity is the determing safety factor in sky sailing. A wind meter is needed to accurately tell the difference between a 10 to 15 mph wind and a 25 to 45 mph wind.
- Never fly in winds that are gusty, downwind, or over 25 mph.
- Do not fly in heavy winds with a sky sail that is bigger than your weight specifications require.
- Check the wind direction at the landing site before you take off.

- The more speed at take-off the better.
- Increase speed over gullys, trees, or canyons. There is no lift in these areas.
- Safety and control are more important than lift.
- Remember that close to the face of a cliff or ridge high turbulence is always present. It can toss the sky sail about like a piece of paper in a wind storm. The most dangerous wind gusts are over 25 mph.
- Never make a high-banked turn unless you have plenty of air speed and altitude.

This basic list is merely a starter. You must make every effort to learn as much as possible about the wind in every area in which you fly.

THE thrill and excitement of sky sailing is available to those who can fly consistently well at their own particular level. A skillful take-off, smooth flight, and graceful landing are all beautiful sights. Whether they are performed at a low ground-skimming level or a high altitude soar makes little difference. Do not allow yourself to be influenced by the actions of other fliers. Every pilot soon learns that he has only himself to account to. Virtually all flying accidents are caused by pilot error. There are many unknowns in the sport of sky sailing—unknowns that can be illuminated only by experience. If you are foolish enough to fly higher than you feel you can handle with confidence, then you are placing your life squarely in the hands of fate. One does not acquire competence and sound flying judgment overnight. These skills are developed in simple steps over a period of time. By developing your flying talents slowly, you are eliminating the possibility of finding yourself in a hazardous flying situation that you cannot handle with confidence.

To the New Pilot

The gradual advance up to higher launching sites is critical to your development as a safe, proficient sky pilot. The smoothness and confidence of your control is essential. Progress slowly and with patience and you will have many memorable flying experiences.

Here are a few things to remember when you are on the hill and have preflight tested the sail:

1. Be familiar with wind direction and speed.
2. Be sure that landing slopes are clear of all obstacles, including spectators.
3. Be sure that the slope has been preflighted without the harness hooked up.
4. Never take off or fly immediately after or behind a sky sail. Wait at least twenty-five or thirty seconds. Sails leave heavy turbulence in their wake and can cause much trouble for the flier who finds himself in the backwash of a sail.
5. Keep your hands on the control bar at all times during flight. If a gust or turbulent air hits the sail, both hands will be needed to guide and control your movement.
6. Always wear your protective clothing.
7. Never fly alone.

Advanced Maneuvers

"B" LEVEL III

NOW that the problems of getting off the ground and landing have been solved, we can move forward to a few more complicated maneuvers. In the earlier lessons the flight of the student pilot was simple. He had only to take off and land. The sail did most of the work. In these lessons he will learn how to more accurately control the sail in its direction to the left and right, up and down, and in landing on a specified spot. The student pilot should not progress any further than this "B" level of flying—seeking higher altitudes, longer flights, or more daring and exciting adventures—until he has mastered these maneuvers. In addition, he will learn a great deal more about the flying qualities of his sail and how to adjust its trim for his specific flying altitudes. Only then should the pilot advance to the "C" flight level of higher altitudes.

Before we move on to higher ground, you should understand what is going to happen there. In these next exercises you will be flying at an altitude that will not exceed 10 to 20 feet, where a mistake in judgment or lack of experience will not be disastrous.

"It is a difficult task to convey to one who has never enjoyed aerial flight a clear perception of the exhilarating pleasure of the elastic motion. The elevation above the ground loses its terror, because we have learned by experience what sure dependence may be placed upon the buoyancy of the air. Gradual increase of the extent of these lofty leaps accustoms the eye to look unconcernedly upon the landscape below. To the mountain climber the uncomfortable sensation experienced in trusting his foot into the slippery notch cut in the ice or to a treacherous rubble above deep abysses, with other dangers of the most terrifying nature, may often tend to lessen the enjoyment of the magnificent scenery. The dizziness caused by this, however, has nothing in common with the sensation experienced by him who trusts himself to the air; for the air demonstrates its buoyancy in not only separating him from the depth below, but also keeping him suspended over it. Resting upon the broad wings of a well-tested flying machine, which, yielding to the least pressure of the body, obeys our directions; surrounded by air and supported only by the wind, a feeling of absolute safety soon overcomes that of danger."

Otto Lilienthal

The launch. Sail-angle of attack neutral—then nose up: the launch should be decisive, strong, and direct. Keep the sail in neutral position until ground and air speed builds up and the sail fills with air.

Launch

FLARE OR PUSH To flare the sail is to move the control bar forward and raise the nose up into a high attack angle. This movement causes the pilot's body to shift back towards the tail of the sail. When a flare maneuver is initiated while in flight the sail will first gain altitude then quickly slow down to a controlled stop, where the wing no longer has any lift and drops to the earth. The flare is used primarily in take-offs and landings.

Keep running until the sail lifts you from the earth.

With the prone harness, bring the legs back and up so that they are level with the body. Notice the wind sock to the rear of the pilot waiting to take off. It is advisable to have a wind direction indicator at the launch site to be able to quickly at a glance notice wind shifts.

NOTE: The student pilot has a tendency to push forward on the bar too soon and too far, causing a stall by having the nose too high. Or the student will pull back too far and too quickly and nose into the hillside. Practice on the gentle slope until the correct launching procedure is mastered.

Once aloft, pull the triangle bar gently towards the belt line to nose down into a dive and build up flying speed.

A Hazardous Launch. This pilot launched at an angle to the wind instead of heading directly into it. As a result of his low flying speed, he is now desperately and dangerously trying to correct his heading back into the wind. Notice his right-hand elbow pointing up in the air as he struggles to get the nose back into the wind. And those cameramen down in front don't help matters. They are in one hell of a position should the flier stall out and crash down. Analysis: Pilot erred in launch and once committed to flight should have lowered his glide angle, flared the kite and quickly landed. It's better to abort a flight with a quick landing and return to the launch area for another try than to attempt to correct a flawed take-off.

NOTE: Winds are fickle. They don't always blow straight up the slope. When winds are blowing up the hill at an angle, you may have to run at that wind angle to launch successfully. Remember: Keep the sail level with the horizon, not the hill, and don't change your attack angle by shifting your direction down the slope. Keep the nose into the wind. A mistake can result in a crash.

Here the pilot makes a proper launch, his feet still pounding the air as the sail lifts him up off the ground. Notice his method of holding the control bar. Many fliers prefer this style over the other two mentioned in this text. All are acceptable. The important thing is to use that style which is the most comfortable for you.

He settles into his prone position. But wait: "What's that line dangling down in the grass?" Should that line snag on anything, it would yank the sail right out of the air and back to earth with a resounding thud. Therefore, allow nothing to dangle or protrude from the sail or your person on a flight.

There are two points to study in this scene. The first is the attack angle of the sail. It should be neutral at this point of the launch. The student (and, again, this is a common mistake) raised the nose up too soon, allowed the wind to get under the sail, and then starts to force it backwards. The student at this point is having a difficult time moving forward. The correct maneuver here would be to lower the bar to the ground, rotate the nose down, and start again.

This sequence illustrates what can happen when the angle of attack of the sail is too high and the launch speed take-off too timid. (This is a typical error most student pilots make on their first attempt, particularly if the wind is a brisk 10–15 mph.) Wing position fine, but the student is not prepared for launch. Notice the position of the feet and the apprehensive expression. At this point, if the student feels the wind is too strong, or if there are other considerations that indicate a less than successful launch, he should put the nose down into the wind and unhook the harness and scrub the flight.

Glide

CONTROL BAR NEUTRAL. BODY CENTERED

The glide is where the real enjoyment of sky sailing is discovered. It is here that the pilot gets a moment to observe his achievement, when poetry is conceived—or fright takes over if the pilot has extended himself beyond his skill. At this point, we can contemplate the original hang gliding chestnut: "Never fly higher than you would like to fall."

After take-off, the control bar is slightly pulled in towards the chest, leveling the sail with the horizon (not the ground), and a stable glide is established where the sail will descend to the ground in its normal glide path. For every 4 feet forward the sail will sink 1 foot down. For a stable glide, the student pilot should not overcompensate his moves by making them too severe. Otherwise, the flight path will resemble a roller coaster ride with a series of ups and down. All movements should be smooth and easy. Small gentle moves should be made to adjust directions. The secret is to stop any tendency to over-control your flight. Remember, it takes a moment for the sail to react to a shift in the body's weight.

Bill Sloatman, of the Chandelle Sky School, executes a left-hand turn. Notice the position of the hands for strong control. The direction of his body adds to the thrust of his turning maneuver.

Notice the dip of the sail to the left. His feet swing over to add additional impetus to the turn.

Left Turn

BODY LEFT   CONTROL BAR RIGHT

All flying directions are oriented from the pilot's position facing towards the nose of the sky sail.

The sky sail turns when one or the other wing is banked either left or right. When the control bar is moved to the left or right, in the air, the body swings to the opposite side of the slide and causes the sail on the weighted side to sink. To make a right turn, slide the bar left across your chest and your body will swing to the right as a counter reaction to your left thrust and vice versa. Turning and banking maneuvers are tricky and should be attempted only after many successful straight line flights. Remember, in

This flier, starting into his left-hand turn, is a brave soul. His protective clothing is nonexistent, and his prone harness arrangement is frightening.

Here you can see the left-hand turn. Right hand sliding the bar over. Left hand well placed and the feet in position. The control bar is centered on his chest.

Note how the pilot has thrust his weight to the right by "straight arming" the control bar to the left.

Here you can see the beginning of the turn. The right-hand wing tip is just starting to dip, and he has swung his legs over and down to create more wind resistance.

BODY RIGHT CONTROL BAR LEFT

Right Turn

all turns increase your speed to prevent a stall. If you are flying close to your minimum speed, make only shallow turns. In preparation for higher altitudes the student pilot must be able to decisively and instinctively master the 90° right- and left-hand turn. This turning skill is required to fly over ridges, to correct headings when making landing approaches, to avoid collisions, and to be able to fly out of unfavorable wind directions.

Turns should only be attempted in a steady, constant wind. Do not attempt a turn in high winds when you are too low or if the wind begins to shift, as it does in the morning or later on in the day.

In this scene you can clearly see the body shift to the right. Note the position of the hands on the control bar.

Viewing the right-hand turn from the rear when the pilot is wearing a prone harness gives a clear picture of the body shift for this maneuver.

The 360° Turn

The pilot has just swung his body right and extended his left arm over against the control bar to start into a right-hand turn. The next sequence of pictures shows the right-hand turn taken to its ultimate conclusion. A 360° full circular turn beautifully executed. The pilot skillfully flew this most difficult maneuver with the skill and precision of a soaring bird. Note, however, by observing the horizon the amount of altitude lost on a turn of this type. The 360° turn should only be performed at a high altitude, in a steady wind, a good distance from the mountains or launch site. When the sail turns and heads back towards the launch site (which is usually the direction from which the wind is blowing), the increase in speed generated by flying downwind will drive the sail back into the mountains, unless there is enough distance and elevation to head back out again.

Notice how the pilot (wearing a seated harness) seems to be hunching over the control bar. What he is doing is pulling the bar back to his midriff so that the nose of the sail will drop down, forcing the sail into a diving attitude. When this happens, the sail will pick up speed, making all the maneuvers easier to manage.

Here you can get a better look at the pullback procedure.
Note his protective clothing. It seems as though he is using the same style protectors as we discussed in the first flight section. A wise decision.

The pilot has just initiated a pullback on the control bar to bring the nose down and increase his air speed.

To dive or to pull is to lower the nose of the sail by pulling the control bar as far back against the body as possible, which shifts the pilot's weight forward towards the nose of the sail. The purpose of the dive is to increase the flying speed of the sail. It is useful to penetrate through strong winds or to gain stable flight in turbulent air.

It may seem paradoxical, but to dive does not necessarily mean to lose altitude. Remember, in the theory of flight, as speed increases so do lift and drag.

Dive

In this closer view, notice the pilot's hand positions on the control bar—a light but positive grip. All the movements, when done properly, require finesse rather than strength.

Landing—control bar full forward, body back. Legs parallel with control bar.

Beautiful body position. Get a good look at the knee hangers attached to his harness. These knee hangers are useful for longer flights.

Here is Bill Sloatman in a flare and a slight left-hand turn combined. He's into his final landing approach.

HERE the pilots are executing the flare maneuver to slow down their flying speed in preparation for landing. They are also correcting their flying direction in order to land precisely on the spot or area they have previously chosen.

There are two types of landings shown here. The first is the preferred landing into the wind, and the second is the more difficult downwind landing (wind on the tail of the sail). Both are shown because there are times when a downwind landing is the only one that can be made at the landing site—for example, if a shift in the wind makes it hazardous to attempt a turn to get one's heading back into the wind. When landing into the wind, zero speed landings are common. But when landing with the wind coming from behind, you'd better be ready to run. A landing of this type requires fifteen or more steps to stop after touchdown.

116

The pilot is really fighting the bar and the sail as he struggles to get the sail over to the left. Notice how he is using his hands to try to shove that bar over— one of his problems is that the nose is too high to attempt a turn. He could stall, which he did and . . .

He came down in the grass far short of his goal, the landing area at the bottom of the hill. Sometimes unplanned landings must be made. Always keep a sharp look for emergency landing areas.

The pilot here on his second run is gently nosing the sail up to slow down for his landing. The angle of his head indicates he will probably turn slightly in that direction.

With the sail in full flare the pilot will settle gently down to a soft landing.

The flier here is really ripping in. His feet are beginning to get ready to start moving the minute he touches down. Note the direction of the wind pennant in the foreground.

The wind has slacked off a little, but it hasn't eased the concern of this flier as he pushes on the bar to flare.

Bill Sloatman flares out and has his heels ready to dig in for a "hot stop." A flier must keep an eye out for those curious spectators who seem to want to get as close to the landing area as possible. After landing, it is wise to warn them how dangerous their position is.

This pilot erred, as many do who wear prone harnesses. They come in too low to the ground before they flare, and the tail of the keel bar digs in before their feet are on the ground.

When this happens, it stops the sail's forward motion and the kinetic energy of the sail, forcing the pilot right down into the turf. The sail should be carefully preflighted for possible damage after such a landing. So should your teeth.

The flier in these two pictures is a moment away from touchdown and has banked the sail to get a little closer to the wind line—not a particularly wise move unless executed by a skilled flier. For the novice, this direction change at the last moment could spell a crash, if that wing tip contacted the ground first. To the right we see a touchdown (and finely executed, as is apparent from the expression on this flier's face). Wing attack angle is correct, as is his body position.

He's coming in a little too fast, and that right-hand wing tip is down.

He held back on the flare, still struggling to get that sail level. I spoke to him after he landed and his comment was, "I was afraid of plowing into the spectators." A wise pilot knows not to land when the landing area is packed with those fearless spectators.

The pilot has the same problem of coming in too low. He's decided to take the landing on his luckily well-padded knees instead of his feet. Practice makes perfect.

Downwind Landings

A pilot may be expert at graduated-slope ground skimming, but flying at high altitudes makes additional demands on both the pilot and his sail. If these demands are not met, they can lead to serious difficulties or injuries.

The Sail: On low-level flights of short duration, the pilot is usually unaware of the precise flying qualities of his sail. It may have a tendency to nose up, down, left, or right. If it does, the pilot will compensate by pushing the control bar in the direction needed to maintain a normal flight path. These slight corrective procedures are acceptable on flights that last less than a minute. But when flying times of several minutes duration are encountered, as they usually are from high elevations, those compensations the pilot has been making to maintain stable flights for his sail can become lethal. The danger is not from equipment malfunction but from pilot exhaustion. High altitude flights of four to five minutes time are not uncommon. If, on one of these flights, the sky sail is out of trim, the pilot must exert pressure on the control bar to compensate for the unevenness. This action requires considerable strength—strength that is rapidly diminished on a long flight, and virtually nonexistent when it is desperately needed to execute the flare in landing. If the pilot is unable to flare, he will plow into the earth at full speed at landing.

A properly trimmed sail is one that flies straight and quietly and responds to gentle touches. If a pilot owns a sail that cannot be adjusted (i.e., keel tube up-reflex, support cable, and control bar adjustment for proper center-of-gravity placement of the pilot), it should never be flown from high altitudes. Sails that are home built or assembled from kits usually need expert attention to align them for proper flying trim. Custom or factory built sails are more easily adjusted.

High Altitude Flying

"C" LEVEL

The Pilot: The flier who launches for the first time from a high altitude suddenly finds himself without a source of orientation. Previously, he had relied upon the speed with which he has moved over the ground, a speed that is easy to determine when he is flying low. When high in the air, the sensation of ground speed is totally absent. The inexperienced pilot who has not learned to fly by gradually working up the slopes is unaware that he is actually flying at a respectable cruising speed. Thinking he has stopped or is about to stall, he pulls the control bar back in and dives to pick up air speed. At a high altitude, with nothing around to orient him to his position, the inexperienced flier can find himself in a full dive before he even realizes it. Several pilots who took off too high too soon have flown right into the ground because they were compensating for something that existed only in their imaginations. This diving syndrome, as it is called in flying, can be avoided by following the escalated-hill learning procedure; that is, only advancing to higher ground after each individual level is thoroughly mastered.

THESE marches up the face of a mountain or the side of a hill give a flier time not only to observe the terrain and wind conditions but also to reflect upon the sport itself and his participation in it. In most cases, on these hiking expeditions there are other fliers along, but there is very little conversation. No matter how experienced a flier is, there is always a slight twinge of anticipation and excitement about the flight. Will I be able to win over the wind, or will it give me trouble? Will I make a mistake and hurt myself? While these doubts remain, the beauty of nature soon takes over: the roll of the terrain, the dome of the sky, the freedom of the clouds, the silence and the solitude. These things remind the flier of how alone he is in this adventure. He surveys the dramatic scene with his sail resting beside him, and the challenge of conquering the air fills him with a sense of awe.

When the summit is reached, the flier concentrates on the business of assembling his sail. The sail—his wings— are an extension of his dreams. Their power is intoxicating and they sometimes overwhelm good judgment. This is the real challenge: to know and respect one's limitations. The wisest fliers know when not to fly and are not embarrassed by making that long hike back to the base with the sail, like a pair of furled wings, resting on their shoulders. The wisdom to wait until another day, when the winds are right and the grip on the control bar perfectly secure, is the wisdom that is born not of weakness but of maturity and strength.

Aloft, the pilot soon begins to realize that the sky sail above him is not a toy and is not to be lightly treated. As he becomes more and more familiar with its personality, quirks, and manners, he begins to think of the sail as an extension of himself, as part of his own bone and muscle, for the winds respond to his every motion. Now that he is in this new environment, the air, he must instinctively develop new responses for situations never before encountered on the earth below. In the same manner that the skindiver has to face the hazards of the deep, the sky sailor must fully understand where aerial danger lurks. His body and mind become sensitive to new sounds: The wind humming on the rigging cables, the flutter of the sail fabric, the hiss of air rushing into the crevasses of his helmet, even the sound of his own heart beating become new, sometimes frightening sensations. In time his new awareness is translated into automatic reactions, as the flier develops skills that will prepare him for the domain of the birds. More important, he develops a special attitude toward his new sport. If he is wise, he forgets the brute-force contact sports he learned on earth and becomes gentle. For now he has joined the ranks of flying creatures. He can look about from his new vantage point and learn new facts about his world.

The flier experiences many new delights as he soars silently across the sky. He takes sharp notice of the way the grass and the trees bend with the ground wind, the way smoke drifts from chimneys, or the way waves ripple across water. These are wind direction signals for the flier to remember in his return to earth. For now the wind is as important to him as the air he breathes. It is his life or death for the duration of his flight.

To fully understand the implications of his new knowledge he must be humble. It was not too long ago that the sky was forbidden territory for man. Mortals who attempted to journey there were thought of by their contemporaries as fools. And when they were destroyed for whatever reason, no one really cared to talk about it; it was the expected fate of the sky voyager. Even today a bit of this skeptic's logic still lurks in each of us, includ-

ing those who strap wings to their vulnerable bodies and take up the challenge of flight. But once they have felt the rush of flying and returned to earth, their lives are irrevocably changed. They have experienced the dangers as well as the exquisite beauty of a new place that was once the exclusive realm of spirits, mythological gods, and feathery creatures. Man's curiosity, wit and perseverance have finally broken the chains of the earth—we have wings, we can fly!

BE

TO BE

FREE AS THE BIRD

SHOULD YOU MAKE YOUR OWN SAIL, OR BUY ONE?

This is a question that constantly arises. Kent Trimble of Manta Products answers this question here in its entirety. . . .

The answer depends on what you want. To save money, make your own. To get one you know will fly well, buy the best available.

It would be extremely unlikely for you to get both values at once, because making a sail is not merely stitching a lot of fabric together. It is a craft that takes years to learn, and no matter how good a seam you can sew you are mistaken if you think you can do as good a job as a master sailmaker. It's not just a question of intelligence, talent, equipment, but the little tricks, the fine points, the master's touch born of experience that makes the difference between mediocrity and high performance. You can prove this to yourself at any flying site . . . closely observe the sails and the performance. You'll find the noisy, flapping sails being out-flown by the smooth, quiet ones, the ones made by pros.

Until you are an advanced pilot able to put a wing through its paces and test the limits of its performance, you have no way to tell a good one from a bad one. Anything that gets a beginner off the ground is great to him, and until he is such an advanced pilot, he will not be able to believe the magnitude of difference in performance between wings that basically look so much alike. But you won't always be a beginner. Sooner or later you're going to want to fly really well. At that point the true cost of making your own sail becomes apparent . . . you've sunk all that time and money into a so-so sail that has only retarded your progress as a flier and now you're faced with having to buy the good one anyway. If you find yourself in this situation, you will find little comfort in the knowledge that you put yourself there when you made your decision months earlier.

If you have the imagination and foresight to look ahead and see yourself reaching for your full potential as a flier, you will not seriously consider making your own sail. You can obtain the finest Rogallo sail made for as little as $140. With reasonable care, it will give you excellent flying for many years. In the long run it is the cheapest way to fly.

On the other hand, if you're a gambler, if you like long shots, if you can see yourself settling for whatever you come up with, make your own. You'll save a few bucks. In the short run, that is.

MANUFACTURERS; ORGANIZATIONS; PUBLICATIONS

If you have enjoyed this book and would like to try sky sailing, I suggest you get in touch with these publications and manufacturers. They are certain to give you sound advice.

SOURCES FOR ULTRALIGHT GLIDERS (PLANS, KITS AND READY-TO-FLY):
Compiled by the United States Hang Gliding Association, Inc., 12536 Woodbine St., Los Angeles, Calif. 90066, phone (213) 397-4848. Prices subject to change without notice.

Rogallo-Type Sky Sails:

Bat-Glider Plans, Box 7115, Amarillo, Texas 79109; plans, $5. Bamboo and plastic. Materials cost can be as little as $20.

Bill Bennett Delta Kites, Box 483, Van Nuys, Calif. 91408, phone (213) 785-2474. Aluminum & Dacron. Ready-to-fly, Model 162 (162" long), $495; Model 186, $595. Kits. Replacement parts available. Write for price list.

Chandelle Corp., c/o Jim Galbreath, 511 Orchard St., Dept. GS, Golden, Colo. 80401, (303) 278-9566. Skysail Rogallo, 15', 16', 18', 20'; kit, $295 (sail unsewn); complete, $395 plus harness. Operates a Skysail School. Write for brochure. So. Calif. rep., Kim Dawson, 2455 Irvine, Costa Mesa, Calif. 92627, (714) 645-2699.

list of schools

CHANDELLE CORPORATION	CHANDELLE UTAH
511 Orchard St.	36980 E. 7000 S.
Golden, Colorado 80401	Salt Lake City, Utah 84121
CHANDELLE WEST (2 schools)	CHANDELLE FORT COLLINS
17815 Sky Park Blvd. #A	c/o Alpine Haus
Irvine, California 92707	628 South College
CHANDELLE SAN FRANCISCO	Fort Collins, Colo. 80521
2123 Junipero Sierra Blvd.	CHANDELLE NORTHWEST
Daly City, California 94015	c/o 2017 Ravenna Blvd. N.E.
CHANDELLE CHICAGO (2 schools)	Seattle, Washington 98105
109 West Prospect	CHANDELLE FRESNO
Mt. Prospect, Illinois 60056	4777 Blackstone
CHANDELLE IDAHO	Fresno, California 93726
P.O. Box 1221	CHANDELLE MARYLAND
Sun Valley, Idaho 83353	5603 McKinley Street
CHANDELLE ARIZONA	Bethesda, Maryland 20034
c/o The Ski Haus, Inc.	
2823 E. Speedway	
Tucson, Arizona 85716	

Mark Chidester, 16603 Covello, Van Nuys, Calif. 9106, phone (213) 994-5834 (or Leo Chidester, 1704 N. Valley View, Layton, Utah 84042, phone (801) 376-9524, or Clive Chidester, Box 1588, Malmstrom AFB, Great Falls, Mont. 59402). Plans and kits (about $250); price list. Sails are of rip-stop nylon.

Cliffhanger, Box 53, Paramount, Calif. 90723, phone (213) 421-7675. Plans, $3; ready-to-fly, $145; polyethylene material kit only, $15. Aluminum-tube structure, 1/16" cable.

Concepts, 1635 Superior Ave., Costa Mesa, Calif. 92627, phone (714) 548-4098. 3 sizes, 16', 18' & 20'. Write for catalog and price list.

Delta Sail Wing Gliders, 501 Westview Dr., Dept. GS, Hastings, Minn. 55033, (612) 437-2685. Span 20', length 14' 7'; plans $19.95 (Ad in 5-73 *Popular Science*, p. 186).

Dunbar Sails, Grove St. Pier, Bldg. A, Oakland, Calif. 94607, (415) 451-4785. Sails only.

Eipper-Formance, Inc., Box 246, Lomita, Calif. 90717, phone (213) 549-4420. Flexi Flier (aluminum & Dacron) plans, $5; also kits and ready-to-fly; hardware, sails & accessories. The Flexi Floater (19' or 20' keel) for heavier pilots, available complete only (plans and kits soon). Write for catalog.

Free-Flight Systems, 10730 Whiteoak, Dept. GS, Granada Hills, Calif. 91344. Plans, $5. Kits, accessories, completed kites. (Ad in 5-73 *Popular Science*, p. 188.)

Hang Craft of San Diego, c/o Wink Saville, 317 Dewey St., #3, Dept. GS, San Diego, Calif. 92113, (714) 453-1910. Plans, kits kites, supplies, consultation.

J & G Aircraft, c/o Jim Diffenderfer, 318 Ramon Dr., Los Altos, Calif. 94022, phone (415) 948-0294. "Ridge Rider," 18' X 16'. Plans, $5. Frame kit, $195.00

Johnson Flex-Wing Kites, c/o Dan Thomson, Box 91, Dept. GS, Cypress Gardens, Fla, 33880, (813) 293-8255. Parts, kits and kites, various sizes. Write for brochure.

Taras Kiceniuk, Jr., c/o Palomar Observatory, Palomar Mtn., Calif. 92060, phone (714) 742-3476. Bamboo & plastic, "Batso" plans, $5.

Kilbourne Sport Specialities, Box 8326, Stanford, Calif. 94305. Kilbo Kite, plans, $15; kit (less sail), $195. Aluminum & Dacron.

William Liscomb, 5735 Grand Ave., Riverside, Calif. 92504, phone (714) 682-7458. Cylindrical booms, 2' wing tip extensions, "Standard Class" (15' booms), 20' keel, aluminum tubing. Plans, $10.

Manta Products, P.O. Box 23272, or 1647 E 14th St., Oakland, Ca. (415) 536-1500. Standard Factory Model 15' thru 20' starts $500. Kits start $315. Accessories Lessons available. Catalogue.

126

Bill Moyes, 12001 Gerald Ave., Granada Hills, Calif. 91334. Aluminum & Dacron, ready-to-fly, about $500.

McBroom Sailwings, Ltd., 12 Manor Court Dr., Dept. GS, Horfield, Bristol 7, England. Write for full details.

Sailbird Flying Machines, 6309 S. Adelia Ave., Dept. GS, Tampa, Fla. 33616. Aluminum and Dacron. Plans, $5; kits, sails, accessories, completed gliders. Free catalog.

Sky Sports, Inc., (M. Markowski & Associates), 542 E. Squantum St., Bldg. 15, Dept. GS, North Quincy, Mass. 02171, (617) 328-1800. Lark, 14', 16' or 18' keel, plans, $6; complete, $480–540. Hark (high aspect ratio, conical), 3 sizes, 138–228 sq. ft.; plans, $7.50; complete, $500–560. Kits, hardware, accessories. Send $1 for catalog.

Seagull Aircraft, 1554 - 5th St., Santa Monica, Calif. 90406, phone (213) 394-4579. Seagull I, II & III (16', 82°; 18', 82°; 18', 100°). Components and complete aircraft. Write for brochure. Plans, $5; ready-to-fly, $420–$480.

Skylark Gliders, 1867 Candle Lane, El Cajon, Calif. 92020. Plans, $4. Wood dowels, plastic pipe and plastic sail.

Sport Kites, Inc., 1201-C E. Walnut, Santa Ana, Calif. 92701, phone (714) 547-1344. "Wills Wing," 18' X 18', Dacron sail, $425 ready to fly.

Ultralight Products (Pete Brock), 137 Oregon St., Dept. GS, El Segundo, Calif. 90245, (213) 322-7171. Plans, $10; custom-built kites, $480–550. Catalog, $2. Specialist in components and hardware.

Velderrain & Co., Box 1946, Los Angeles, Calif. 90028, phone (213) 542-4153. Aluminum tubes, plastic sails. Plans, $4. Ready-to-fly, $175.00 to $200.00, plus shipping. Price list available.

Whitney Enterprises, Box 90762, Los Angeles, Calif. 90009, phone (213) 641-5303. Aluminum tubes, 18' booms, 20' keel. 32-page plan set, $7.50. Porta-Wing, 20' keel, 18' cable cylindrical leading edges, breaks down to a 5' x 1' x 1' package, $550. Also, Dacron sails available.

Biplanes:

Seagull Aircraft, 1554 - 5th St., Dept. GS, Santa Monica, Calif. 90401, (213) 394-4579. Waterman/Seagull Classic Biplane; 2-axis control (elevator, interplane spoilers, dihedral), weighs 60 lb. Plans, $5. Materials kits later.

Ultralight Flying Machines, Box 59, Cupertino, Calif. 95014, phone (408) 732-5463. Kit for Icarus II tailless, $395 (less fabric), plus shipping. Includes plans. Write for brochure.

Taras Kiceniuk, Jr., c/o Palomar Observatory, Palomar Mtn., Calif. 92060, phone (714) 745-3476. Icarus II tailless, plans, $10. Weight, 55 lb.

Jack Lambie, 9460-E Artesia, Bellflower, Calif. 90706, phone (213) 925-6040. Plans for "Hang Loose" Chanute-type biplane, wood, wire and plastic, $3.

Volmer Aircraft, Box 5222, Dept. 8, Glendale, Calif. 91201. Plans for J-11 "SO-LO", Chanute-type, full controls, $30; info pkg. & photo, $2.

Monoplanes:

Frank Colver, 3076 Roanoke Lane, Costa Mesa, Calif. 92626, phone (714) 546-9647. Plans for flying wing model of full-size CW-1, with info on it, $2.

Eipper-Formance, Inc., Box 246, Lomita, Calif. 90717, phone (213) 549-4420. Cronkite, a cylindrical, high-aspect-ratio Rogallo, plans, $5; Quicksilver monoplane (successor to the Hightailer), plans, $5; also kits & ready-to-fly for both; hardware, sails & accessories. Write for catalog.

Mike Flannigan, 20560 Summerville, Excelsior, Minn. 55331. Flannigan Sailwing, drawings, materials list and description, $3. A flying wing with swept back. Aluminum and polyethelene.

Jim Spurgeon, 5590 Morro Way, La Mesa, Calif. 92041. Plans for John Montgomery's 1883 hang glider, $5.

Volmer Aircraft, Box 5222, Dept. 8, Glendale, Calif. 91201. Plans for "Swingwing," wood, fabric, metal-tube construction, $50. Info kit, $2.

Ornithopters:

Pteryx Machine, 7350 Atoll Ave., Unit 7, North Hollywood, Calif. 91605, phone (213) 764-1600. Man-carrying ornithopters, ultralight sailplanes, machine shop services. Exploded ornithopter drawing and price list, 22 X 28 poster size, $2 postpaid. Also, "I Want To Fly Like a Bird" poster, $2, postpaid. See page 49.

ORGANIZATIONS

Boston Sky Club, Box 375, Marlboro, Mass. 01752, phone (617) 485-5740. Annual dues, $6, includes subscription to bimonthly newsletter, *SKY-SURFER*.

Self-Soar Assn., Box 1860, Santa Monica, Calif. 90406. No dues (sign form).

Southern California Hang Glider Association, Inc., c/o Chuck Kocsis, Jr., 12328 Otsego St., North Hollywood, Calif. 91607, phone (213) 762-

4774. Annual dues, $3, includes subscription to monthly publication, *GROUND SKIMMER*. Over 800 members. Meets monthly in Los Angeles (call 390-4440 for date).

Wings of Rogallo, c/o Gary Warren, 502 Barkentine Lane, Redwood City, Calif. 94065, phone (415) 592-1908. Annual dues, $5, includes subscription to monthly newsletter.

PUBLICATIONS

DELTA KITE FLYER NEWS, Box 483, Van Nuys, Calif. 91408, phone (213) 785-2474. Three issues printed to date. Subscription price, $3.50/year.

GROUND SKIMMER, c/o Lloyd Licher, Editor, 12536 Woodbine St., Los Angeles, Calif. 90066, phone (213) 397-4848. Monthly publication of the Southern Calif. Hang Glider Assn., began in May, 1972. Subscription included in membership; annual dues, $3. Attempting to cover history of the ultralight movement as it happens, plus articles and photos of new aircraft, materials, sources, bibliography, safety, flying activity, etc.

LOW & SLOW, Box 1860, Santa Monica, Calif. 90406, $6/yr.

SKYSURFER, Box 375, Marlboro, Mass. 01752, phone (617) 485-5740. Newsletter of the Boston Sky Club, included with membership; annual dues, $6. Bimonthly. Began June, 1972.

TRUE FLIGHT, 1719 Hillsdale Ave., San Jose, Calif. 95124. A 47-page book for $5, includes drawings for Dave Kilbourne's Rogallo hang glider, sources, recommendations, instructions for flying, safety, sails, and numerous photos.

WINGS OF ROGALLO-NEWSLETTER, 1137 Jamestown Drive, Sunnyvale, Calif. 94037. $5 yearly subscription.

NEW ORGANIZATIONS

Canada - Willi Muller (Box 4063 Postal Station "C," Calgary, Alberta, Canada T2T 5M9) is working on the idea of getting a Canadian hang glider association started. He is one of Canada's most active Rogallo pilots.

Oregon - Mike Moore (1729 Labona Dr., Eugene, Oregon 97401) has helped form the Oregon Hang Gliding Association and is its first Vice President. OHGA put on a flying demonstration for the public and press at Cape Kiwanda near Lincoln City in early April, 1974.

CLUBS

Delta Birdmen, c/o Lance Leonard, 147 N. Wilcox Ave., Los Angeles, CA 90038. PH 886-7825.

Eastern Penn Hang Glider Assoc., c/o J. M. McTammany, 620 Walnut St., Reading, PA 19601.

Michigan Skysurfers, c/o Mark Richards, 1361 Oregon, Pontiac, MI 48054. PH 681-4017.

New England Ridge Rider Assoc., 274 Bishops Terr., Hyannis, MA 02601. PH 775-3898.

North American Sky Sailing Association, c/o Bob Jensen, Chandelle Corporation, 511 Orchard Street, Golden, Colorado 80401.

North Carolina Hang Glider Society, c/o Tommy Thompson, 104 Wright St., Lewisville, NC 27023.

Oregon Hang Gliding Assoc., c/o Dave Miller, 829 NE Imperial, Portland, OR 97232.

So-Lo Hang Glider Club, c/o Dan Schmitz, 209 Ninth Ave, Hiawatha, IA 52233.

Utah Ultralight Gliders Assoc., c/o Keith Halls, 143 E 500 N, Kaysville, UT 84037.

Wisconsin Self-Soaring Assoc., 515 Milwaukee Ave, South Milwaukee, WI 53172.

There are two instances in which a waiver of legal rights may be requested. Frequently a student pilot at a school of instruction will be asked to sign a waiver. Equally important, a flyer should carry with him a waiver of the type illustrated here when he asks permission to use an owner's property as a flying site.

Waiver of Legal Rights

I hereby acknowledge that I will take full responsibility for any injury that I may suffer while on your property. I further acknowledge any legal rights that may accrue as the result of any injury I may suffer while flying my "hang glider" on or across your property, and having acknowledged such rights I hereby waive them and any other legal rights related thereto.

This constitutes a waiver of my rights and is an agreement that I will not pursue any other legal remedies. I further agree that I will limit my use of the land to flying my "hang glider," and I agree to use the land only at such time as may be designated.

Having considerable experience flying a "hang glider," I have the ability to determine where and how to fly the "hang glider" under any given conditions, thereby minimizing the possibility of any injury. DATE . . . , NAME . . .

FEDERAL AERONAUTICAL ASSOCIATION

The administration of the F.A.A. has ruled that hang gliding, sky sailing is comparable to sport parachute jumping making only brief use of air space so it will not be subject to F.A.A. regulations. It does, however, feel it should regulate the rigid wing bi- and mono-planes.

Bill Allen, the Editor of *Ground Skimmer* magazine, feels . . .that the future of hang gliding will inevitably depend on our accident rate and the manner in which we deal with property owners, police, and government agencies regulating aircraft? That most police are friendly to the sport and the Federal Aviation Agency probably won't exercise jurisdiction unless we force them to?

. . . that if the F.A.A. does take jurisdiction over the new sport, most "home-made" or "kit" hang gliders will probably not meet the inevitable Federal standards, and the cost of commercially manufactured kites will probably go up?

Towed sky sails also enter into the picture of F.A.A. regulatory powers.

PHOTO CREDITS

Rick Carrier - Layout, art and design. All photos taken by the author, Cannon F.1. Photos on pages 1,7,8,10,26,37,43 (top), 45,60,62,66 (through) 75, 80 (through) 98, 103, 104, 105, 109, 110 (bottom), 111 (bottom), 112 (through) 119, 122, 123, 126, 127.

Chandelle - For the many technical photos and the use of their personnel and facilities at Golden Colorado.

Lynn Ramsey - 2,3,31,35,36 (upper right), 37,38,44,46,48,49,63,77 (top), 78 (bottom), 85 (frame) 2,102 (frame), 1,2,5,6,7,8,104,105 (background photo), 105 lower bottom and center right, top row) 108, 111 (top two) 112 (lower left) 113 (lower right), 117 (bottom) 124.

Peter Menzel - Endpapers, 5,32,44,77 (bottom), 100,101,125.

Peter Brock - 36,64,84 (frame 13), 102 (frame 10), 120, 121.

Jeanine Brock - 32A

David Esler - 30,34.

J.G. Aircraft - 25,29,33 (top left), 78 (top).

R. Rassmussen - 33 (bottom left).

Gordon Lemon - 44 (bottom), 50, 51, 110 (top).

Bill Bennett - 54,56,104 (lower top left), 105 (upper top right)

Mike Robertson - 55,57.

Eiper Formance - For Drawings - 41,50,51. Photos - 102 (Frame 9).

Paramount Pictures Corporation and the producers of *Jonathan Livingston Seagull* - 6,58,59,99 (background), 114.

TYPOGRAPHY

This book was set in English and Claro on Alphatype equipment by University Graphics, Inc., Shrewsbury, New Jersey. The camera conversions were supervised by Vincent Lipert with Neil Deckert, Bill Anderson and Gerry Griffin. Make-up, keyboarding and reading were done by the staff and personnel of University Graphics, Inc.

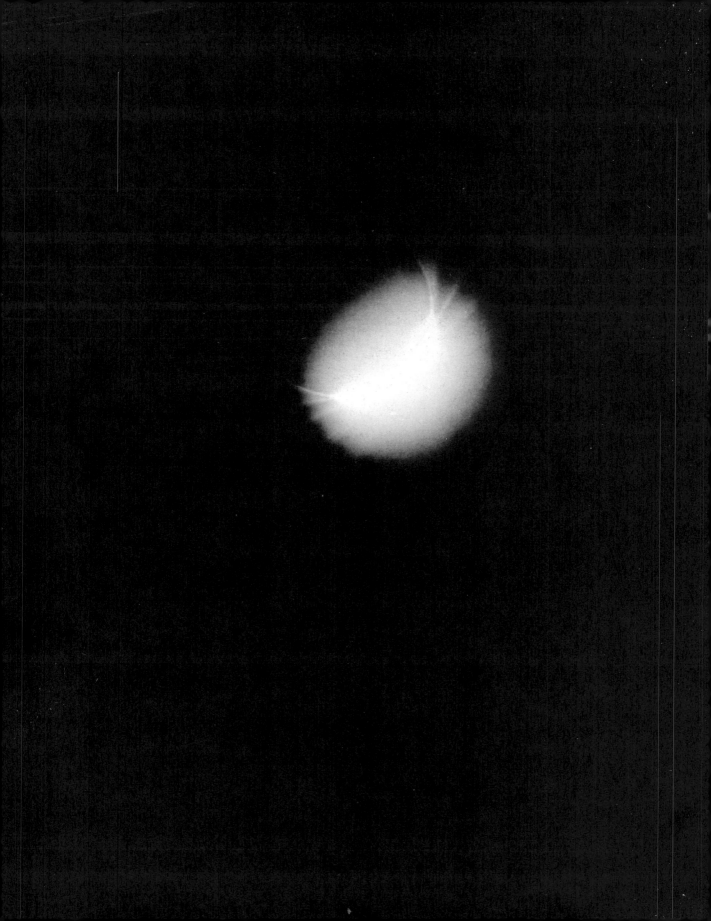